SHEFFI
ARMOURER TO THE
BRITISH EMPIRE

Stewart Dalton

Wharncliffe Books

ACKNOWLEDGEMENTS

The author wishes to acknowledge the assistance given to him by Sheffield Libraries Archives and Information, Rotherham Libraries, Local Studies Department, Sheffield Industrial Museums Trust, R.C.A.F Museum, Trenton, Marconi PLC, Edgar Allen Ltd. and Sheffield Newspapers Ltd.

The following individuals kindly assisted with the illustrations: Harold Edwards, Sheila Shaw, Edgar Gilert, Lorraine Mawson, Phillip Jubb, William Ferguson Jnr. and Ian Faraday.

First Published in 2004 by
Wharncliffe Books
an imprint of
Pen and Sword Books Limited,
47 Church Street, Barnsley,
South Yorkshire. S70 2AS

Copyright © Author 2004

For up-to-date information on other titles produced under the Wharncliffe imprint, please telephone or write to:

Wharncliffe Books
FREEPOST
47 Church Street
Barnsley
South Yorkshire S70 2BR
Telephone (24 hours): 01226 - 734555

ISBN: 1-903425-13-1

A CIP catalogue record of this book is available from the British Library

Printed in the United Kingdom by
CPI UK

CONTENTS

Other Local Titles

The Making of The South Yorkshire Landscape
Melvyn Jones
ISBN: 1-871647-75-4
£9.95

Lost Theatres of Sheffield
Bryen D. Hillerby
ISBN: 1-871647-53-3
£9.95

Aspects of Sheffield
Melvyn Jones
ISBN: 1-871647-40-1
£9.99

Aspects of Sheffield 2
Melvyn Jones
ISBN: 1-871647-58-4
£9.95

Industrial South Yorkshire in Pictures
Paul Walters & Giles Brierley
ISBN: 1-871647-43-6
£7.99

Please contact us via any of the methods below for more information or a catalogue.

WHARNCLIFFE BOOKS
47 Church Street – Barnsley – South Yorkshire – S70 2AS
Tel: 01226 734555 – 734222 Fax: 01226 724438
E-mail: enquiries@pen-and-sword.co.uk – Website:
www.wharncliffebooks.co.uk

PREFACE

On 11th November 1918, the guns of the first Great War of the twentieth century fell silent. For the preceding four years its chief participants had spread the war globally in their search for victory and yet, when the Germans sued for peace, their armies remained almost entirely, upon occupied territory. The belief by the German Army that they had been 'let down' by those at home, coupled with a series of punitive measures by the Allies, ensured that the likelihood of a further European war became a strong possibility.

The wish of many Germans for a revision of the settlement, which would rectify the perceived injustices as well as restoring national pride, would eventually find a voice in political leaders all too eager and willing to act. That the United States Congress did not accept President Wilson's political dreams and plans for a world at peace with itself merely exacerbated the situation and added to the inevitability of a 'continuation' war. The burden of blame for the Second World War must lie with the politicians who failed to create a satisfactory settlement for Europe following the 'war to end wars'.

Much has been written about the outbreak of the First World War; of the jingoism and the widespread lack of understanding as to the enormity of the likely suffering and cost, both in lives and of finance for those who would participate in it. Still more has been written about the campaigns of the Second World War but less attention has been paid to the vast majority of the population who, whilst staying at home, and solely out of national need, contributed to the nation's hard won success in both bloody conflicts. This book then, is as much about the country's working people, who proved their patriotism beyond any doubt, as it is about the entrepreneurs whose factories produced the weapons, which eventually secured victory.

Chapter One

The Area and its People – Summer 1914

The First World War, and more particularly its Western Front, carving its way inexorably across southern Belgium and northern France, came to symbolise, for many, the brutality of total war. A characteristic feature, throughout, was the increasing application of modern science and technology to both defensive and offensive weaponry. These technological advances allowed for the possibility of inflicting bodily injury and damage on a hitherto unheard of scale. The industrial complexes producing these weapons were controlled, throughout Europe, by a small number of large armaments manufacturers. For the British Empire the majority of these companies were closely associated with an area of Yorkshire, perhaps best known by its old name of Hallamshire centred on Sheffield and its smaller, yet equally important neighbour, Rotherham.

Almost five years earlier and before Britain fell into the abyss of war, 1914 had dawned upon Sheffield's grim industrial valleys with

Queen Victoria opening Sheffield Town Hall. By using a ceremonial lock and key coupled to an electrical current, she never left her carriage. (Sheffield Libraries, Archives and Information, S 03513, with permission)

the City looking forward to becoming a See in its own right and having its first bishop. An Order in Council creating Hedley Burrows the first Bishop of Sheffield, fuelled a flourishing civic and municipal pride and confirmed the city's growing importance on the national stage. It already had its own university, established by Royal Charter in 1905, but the imposing Town Hall, built in stone, marble and gilt and opened by Queen Victoria herself in her Diamond Jubilee year of 1897, signalled the city's municipal aspirations.

Sheffield, according to those who enjoyed the benefits of its prosperity gained as a result of human skill in the working of metals, could be summed up as, 'dull and uninspiring, but well run.' Three bullion dealers, five financial agents and a host of banks served the business community, whilst nine shipping lines and almost as many agents operating out of the city arranged the export of Sheffield's products around the globe. Indeed such was its stature in terms of world trade that the consulates or vice consulates of some sixteen nations including those of major European and world powers such as the USA, France, Germany and Russia were located there. Much of the trade was in armaments and Britain's involvement in the world's arms trade was so extensive that it was estimated that in 1913, the last year of peace, 63% of the world trade in naval weaponry emanated from Britain.

The Sheffield of 1914 was, however, a divided city. Many of those whose skills contributed to its prosperity did not reap its benefits. It was a place of those who 'had' and those who 'had not'. Out of a population of some 454,632 souls as recorded in the census of 1911, only 69, 807 were eligible to vote. A large proportion of the industrial workers lived in grim, squalid conditions of which the 260 dwellings housing 1,260 men women and children known as The Crofts (Sims Croft, Hawley Croft, School Croft and Lee Croft) were a typical example. In these poor, grossly overcrowded and unsanitary areas, illness and premature death were commonplace. Infant mortality was high – there were only 53 midwives practising in the whole of Sheffield – with only 66% of children surviving their first few years.

The Crofts were one of the first areas to be demolished by the fledgling City Council, which had been created by an Act of Parliament some twelve years earlier. The newly erected, model workman's homes' around Hawley Street stood as testament to the aspirations and good intentions of Sheffield's council towards its less fortunate citizens.

On the other hand the city had over 1000 insurance agents who collected the premiums to provide healthcare for those who could

ADMIRAL COUNT H. TOGO AND SUITE
EAST HECLA WORKS
HADFIELDS L^{TD} SHEFFIELD.
JULY 20TH, 1911.

British involvement in building the Japanese fleet was immense. Here an official delegation is photographed during a visit to Hadfield's prior to World War One. (Sheffield Libraries, Archives and Information, 623.4 SSTQ, with permission)

afford it and, in a world without radio or television, there was no lack of venues such as the Lyceum, the two Theatres Royal, The Albert Hall and the Hippodrome in which the populace could seek their entertainment. In addition, there were upwards of twenty private clubs and numerous political organisations representing differing interests and political persuasions. The political climate of the time was one in which universal suffrage had yet to be won, Irish expectations of Home Rule were high and an infant Labour Party could not necessarily count on the support of the whole of the labouring class whilst those who represented the forces of conservatism were being challenged to recognise the growing demands for human and civil rights. As the war clouds gathered above the City of Steel towards the end of July 1914, however, the voices urging reform were beginning to be drowned out by the

Numbers 5, 6 and 1, Court Number 8, Furnace Hill. Typical examples of Sheffield's slum housing. (Sheffield Libraries, Archives and Information, U 00726, with permission)

clarion calls of patriotism and duty and the need to service the British war 'machine'.

All of these individuals and undertakings would, to some degree, be put to the test in servicing the industrial war machine that would increase with the scale of destruction on the battlefields. That destruction would amount to the deaths of over eight and a half million members of humankind and the mutilation of thousands more in a conflict between nations of similar ethnic background, to say nothing of family links between their monarchies. It was a war that would last for over four years and ultimately, would involve sixteen nations. None of this could possibly have been envisaged by any of the European powers in the summer of August 1914. It was to Hallamshire's factories, large and small, that Britain and her Empire would turn in her hour of greatest need.

By constructing and using weapons, humankind has gained a fearsome ability to harm its members far beyond that of any other animal. In the case of nations and states, the legitimate use of weapons has typically been in relation to the pursuit or defence of political and economic ends.

As technology evolved, so too did the sophistication of weapons built in conjunction with a ready supply of mass-produced steel. It was steel, in large quantities, which was needed to make the weapons that would dominate the battlefields of the first half of the twentieth century. Nations sought to keep abreast of arms developments and the market for weaponry became huge and profitable. Industry and commerce became willing partners in the race to create ever more powerful and efficient means of destruction.

The Sheffield area's role in this process began hundreds of years earlier by producing arrowheads and cutting weapons such as swords and daggers. However, the introduction of gunpowder and the development of cannons revolutionised warfare. Hand in hand with this revolution came the quest for reliable materials, which would be capable of withstanding the explosive pressures caused by firing the gunpowder, enabling projectiles to be directed towards the enemy rather than having weapons explode in the faces of those firing them. Bronze was the normal medium but was expensive to make and England was largely reliant upon the Flemish manufacturers. King Henry VIII, who was often short of finance, began the quest for self-sufficiency in the supply of cannons. He wanted them made from cheaper and more readily available iron. Foundry techniques slowly developed in many iron-working parts of the kingdom including South Yorkshire. By the late eighteenth century, Rotherham's Samuel Walker, whose works were in Masboro, was casting cannons: producing most of those used by Wellington in the Peninsular War. A little further afield, in northeast Derbyshire, the Sitwell's produced large quantities of cannon balls for the Royal Navy at their Renishaw foundry. It is perhaps with the 'Senior Service' that the area's position as a major arsenal became established. With cannons becoming ever more powerful and sophisticated so the inherent weakness of timber to withstand the impact of their projectiles encouraged experiments in cladding ships' hulls with iron plates.

The age-old race between projectile and armour thus entered another phase with arms manufacturers devoting prodigious amounts of energy in researching and developing offensive weapons and defensive counter measures. It was generally acknowledged in Sheffield, that, *"On one side of the road someone is inventing an armour plate that will resist the most formidable piercing shell made ... [whilst] an establishment on the other side is producing a shell against which nothing can possibly stand".*[1]

Britain's ancient enemy, France, had not seriously threatened naval supremacy since the Napoleonic Wars but there was some considerable disquiet within the Admiralty, when, in 1857, it learned that the French were laying down a series of ironclad battleships, the prototype of which was the *Gloire*. She was designed to withstand the impact of a 50lb muzzle loaded shell and had armour plating of between 4.3 and 4.7 inches thick. These iron plates were produced by forging which, as a method, restricted their dimensions. Naturally, the Admiralty reacted to this naval scare and the *Warrior and Black Prince*, each carrying 4.5-inch armour, were built in response.

Both Samuel Beale and Co. at the Park Gate works and John Brown and Company's Atlas Works rolled armour plates. The major

An advertisement for Cammel Laird and Co. Ltd., c. 1900. It clearly shows the shipyards at Birkenhead as well as the Sheffield works. (Sheffield Libraries, Archives and Information, S 09739, with permission)

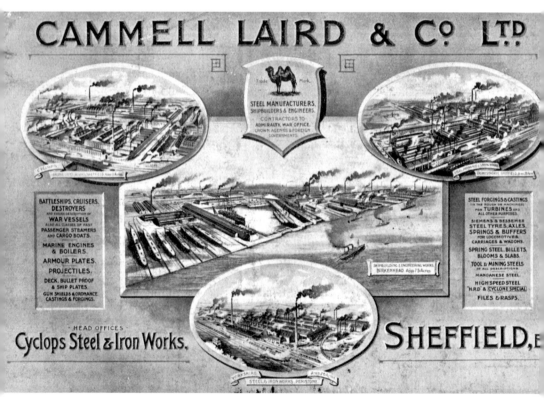

Forgings for a 13.5-inch naval gun at Cammel Laird during World War One.
(Sheffield Libraries, Archives and Information, 338.4, with permission)

advantage of rolling, rather than forging plates, was that much larger and more accurate plates could be manufactured. The other advantage was that they could be manufactured more quickly and thus more cheaply. From these beginnings, Sheffield and Rotherham would grow to become the world's most significant area for the production of naval armour. Vickers, Thos. Firth, John Brown, Hadfield's and Cammell-Laird all invested huge amounts of resources to ensure they retained their technological lead.

The iron and steel works of the Sheffield region met not only domestic but also a world demand for a vast range of engineering and allied products. This industrial infrastructure was also a pre-requisite for the supply of the other aspects of the military problem of piercing armour plate; namely, projectiles and guns. A gun barrel was required which would withstand the enormous pressures built up by the explosive forces of the propellant and the projectile itself needed to have sufficient integrity so as not to burst within the barrel. Vickers forged the early Armstrong gun barrels, as tubes, at their River Don Works and shells were produced by a number of local companies. Improvements in the quality of armour plate had the effect of increasing its resistance to penetration. This advance was met by the

The forge at Hadfield's East Hecla works. A steam hammer and re-heating furnaces are clearly visible. (Sheffield Libraries, Archives and Information, S 09856, with permission)

use of more powerful, explosive propellants allowing for higher muzzle velocities. With higher velocities and the use of capped projectiles came an increase in penetrative power. The quality of the product was vital and Sheffield's reputation was built upon the metallurgical integrity of its products.

In the early 1900s Douglas Vickers, a family member and director of Vickers Son and Maxim, estimated that, *"over a few years, armour resistance had increased by 200 %, whilst the effectiveness of shells increased by approx. 135%".*[2]

A typical 12-inch naval shell of 1905 vintage, when tested, was quite capable of penetrating a 12-inch cemented armour plate backed by three feet of oak and 1inch of skin plate and even remained intact after going through 30 feet of sand. The test projectile in question was recovered some 120 yards from the test butts! These advances were only made possible by thorough research, development and expensive investment in plant and equipment. Naturally, the Admiralty was required to support these advances, not only financially, but also by the awarding of large contracts. Indeed, it established its own presence in the city to oversee these contracts. The Engineers' Office was established at 123, Surrey Street and the Inspection Office on Janson Street. This latter establishment would live on until the 1970s, and for some older Sheffielders, Janson Street, will always be known as *"t Admirality"*.

Britain's Army in 1914 was numerically small but generally considered to be highly professional, existing, unlike those of continental Europe, without the need for compulsory military service. It numbered less than a quarter of a million men and was spread across

MODERN ARMOUR-PIERCING SHELL

I. AND II. METHOD OF SECURING CAPPED SHOT
III. SHOT AFTER PENETRATING KRUPP ARMOUR.

An array of armour piercing shells. (Sheffield Libraries, Archives and Information, 338.4, with permission)

the globe. Annual expenditure amounted to less than £ 29 million, compared with the Navy's budget of over £ 51 million. The army was gradually shedding the scandals of earlier years, during which rank and privilege had proved to be more important than ability in terms of promotion. Its role was to protect the financial interests that had accrued as a result of Empire. Since 1815 Britain's stance had developed into one that sought to avoid military involvement on the continent. Consequently, the War Office was totally unprepared for the magnitude of events that were to unfold on the Western Front and urgent demands for hitherto unheard of quantities of munitions, men and guns of all calibres, were to be made of industry. It is hardly surprising that these demands by both the Admiralty and War Office created industrial chaos.

Heavy shells awaiting dispatch at Hadfield's Ltd. (Sheffield Libraries, Archives and Information, 623.4, with permission)

Hadfield's shells and an armour plate test piece showing the effects of armour piercing shot. (Sheffield Libraries, Archives and Information with permission)

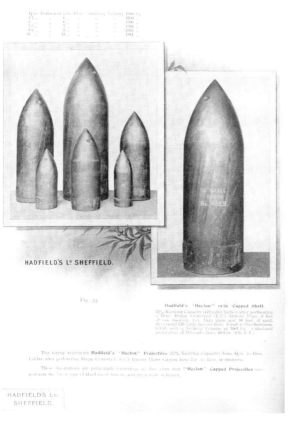

HADFIELD'S Lᵈ SHEFFIELD.

Fig 33.

Hadfield's 'Heclon' 12 in Capped Shell.

Promotional leaflet for Hadfield's 'Heclon' projectiles. (Sheffield Libraries, Archives and Information with permission)

When war broke out Sheffield had a male work force of well over 100,000, of whom 70% would remain at work throughout the war, being over age for military service, engaged in very skilled work or deemed to be medically unfit. One shock, highlighted by the war, was the revelation of the extent of medical unfitness for even basic military service of great numbers of working class men. A poor diet and poor living and working conditions had taken their toll and this problem would continue to engage the authorities as they tried to balance the conflicting demands for manpower in both the armed forces and industry.

In December 1914, it was estimated that 75% of Sheffield's industries were engaged in arms manufacture and were consequently very busy, yet one traditional Sheffield trade quickly ran into difficulties. The war caused a dramatic reduction in sales of high-quality cutlery and silver products and together with a scarcity of labour, this placed Sheffield's 1,600 cutlers in serious difficulties. Despite moves toward war work as diverse as producing flechettes (lethal, sharpened steel darts, dropped from aircraft onto infantry below) swords, razors, surgical instruments and cooking utensils the trade was, in the long term, irreparably damaged. As it slowly realised Sheffield's productivity limitations, government orders were placed with the U.S.A. for razors and pocket-knives at prices and at rates of delivery which the Sheffield cutlers could only

7-IN. KRUPP ARMOUR, AFTER ATTACK BY 10-IN. SHELL.

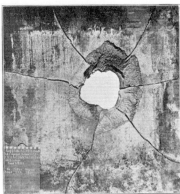

9-IN. KRUPP ARMOUR, AFTER ATTACK BY 13.5-IN. SHELL.

German Krupp armour showing the destruction wrought by various calibres of shell. (Sheffield Libraries, Archives and Information with permission)

dream of. Whilst the heavy engineering trades had invested heavily in modern plant the cutlers had, in general, failed to keep abreast of technology.

Chapter Two

Armageddon

Sheffield's armaments manufacturers had benefited over the years from considerable metallurgical research and demand for their superior products grew as the war progressed. Sheffield's advanced materials assisted in the development of aviation technology and the introduction of the armoured tank. Its steel would see service in products ranging from the British Tommy's steel helmet and bayonet to the massive armour plate and the heaviest naval shells that enabled Britain's warships to contest control of the seas. Sheffield already possessed the industrial plant, infrastructure and an experienced work force. It was to become the British Empire's major arsenal and as the war effort grew so would the size and profitability of Sheffield's major companies.

Table 1. Growth in Issued Capital of Sheffield's Major Steel Companies 1914–1919

	1914	1919
	£	£
Vickers	7,015,000	20,663,237
John Brown	3,573,000	4,187,500
Cammell-Laird	2,372,895	4,018,416
Hadfield's	700,000	1,900,000
Thos. Firth	520,000	1,600,000

To enable this crisis driven growth, significant increases in the numbers of the labour force were essential. Initially, the national and local reservoirs of the unemployed were engaged in the factories, "After five months of war only a thousand out of a population of nearly half a million remain unemployed", remarked the *Sheffield Independent* on 9th January 1915. Other workers arrived from abroad; Belgian refugees and Canadians bolstered the ever-growing army of factory workers and after 1915 increasing numbers of women found war work, especially in the shell shops. Nationally, July 1914 saw some 212,000 women working in what would become known as the munitions industries and by the last year of the war this number had grown to nearly 920,000. These women, nicknamed "munitionettes", came from all over the country and from many walks of life. Living away from home, perhaps for the first time, as well as possessing the high wages munitions work paid, gave them a freedom and independence they had never before experienced. This gave rise to an unparalleled degree of social change; a change frequently frowned upon! It was not only women who found their way into factories from backgrounds alien to industrial life; many men, of widely varied experience and often considered unfit for military service, were employed in South Yorkshire's weapons workshops.

One of these new workers was Septimus Arthur Bennett, ceramic artist and poet, and the younger brother of Arnold Bennett the notable author. In early 1915, he offered his services to the Vickers Company and they found him employment as a trainee lathe operator at their Holme Lane Works. His initial reaction to Sheffield, recorded in his diary, was far from flattering. "Belching furnaces, the rumbling noises of hidden machinery, the hissing of steam over black pools of water, the vast prison-like places employing seven, eight or even ten thousand hands, makes me shudder to think of having to work among such surroundings, not to mention living there", he observed.[1] His description of Sheffield's, "black satanic mills" probably echoes accurately what any sensitive person might observe

A group of 'munitionettes' pose for the camera. (D. S. Dalton)

Bankfield Road, Malin Bridge, S6. Septimus Bennett lodged here during his time as a munitions worker. (D.S. Dalton)

for the first time of an area dedicated to metal working and production.

These new workers needed housing in an area already desperately short of housing stock. Arthur Bennett lodged, for three years, with the Burnley family who lived on Bankfield Road in nearby Malin Bridge, close to the Holme Lane Works.

With insufficient lodgings for the large numbers of new munitions workers flooding into the area, hostels and hutted camps had to be established urgently in the main manufacturing areas. The huts on Tyler and Petre Streets, with their three social halls, were built in 1916 for the Ministry of Munitions. Rented out at 6/6d per week, the wooden quarters were situated away from the mainstream of urban life and being thus isolated and largely self-contained, became a source of some notoriety and urban myth.

Mark Firth – Sheffield born and ultimately one of its benefactors – and his brother had founded Thos. Firth and Company in 1842. They and their father Thomas, who joined them some months later, were not untypical of the Sheffield steel masters of the time in that they took out of the business less than they had previously been earning and invested the rest in so as to ensure the new company's success. The company had soon entered the profitable arms industry and was already a well-established military and naval supplier when war broke out. During the conflict, it alone manufactured over four million shells of varying sizes that were, eventually, being produced at a rate of two shells per minute. It also completed over 9,000 tons of gun forgings, ranging from the $1^1/_2$-inch anti-aircraft to the 15-inch naval guns, capable of firing an armour piercing projectile weighing 1,910 lbs over 30 miles. Other naval work accounted for 10,000 tons of marine shafts and turbine forgings, including those for H.M.S. *Colossus* and the White Star liners *Olympic* and *Titanic*. By the end of the war, the company employed over 5,000 women workers in its purpose built shell factory at Templeborough, together with an additional 2,500 women engaged in war work at other plants in the area.

Another company founded by a local man was Hadfield's. Robert Abbott Hadfield had been born in 1858 in Sheffield's Attercliffe district and he had set up his own, small foundry in 1872. From these relatively humble beginnings, the company grew rapidly and by 1914 was a world leader in its field with a workforce of 5,980 employed at their new, purpose built, East Hecla Works. They possessed the most extensive foundry of its kind in the world and were, pre-war, the biggest manufacturer of both artillery and naval gun projectiles of all sizes. Their considerable pre-war research and development of ballistics and manufacturing technologies had allowed perfection of the production of cast steel projectiles. These had the same metallurgical integrity as those produced by forging and their development of projectile caps had significantly increased the destructive capacity of the projectiles to which they were fitted.

During the war, apart from vast quantities of steel projectiles, they also produced other items including guns, gun shields, armour plate,

Sheffield's East End. The notorious wooden munitions workers' huts on Petre Street.
(Sheffield Libraries, Archives and Information, S 12659, with permission)

howitzers, trench mortars and latterly, tank tracks, as well as the tough manganese steel which was used for soldier's helmets. As the war progressed they organised a completely new shell factory within their own works, as well as greatly boosting their steel melting facilities to meet the urgent demand for supplies

By 1918, Hadfield's was one of the area's biggest employers, with a work force that had grown to almost 15,000, of whom 500 were women. They were also the nation's largest special alloy steel manufacturer.

Charles Cammell moved to Sheffield from Hull in the 1830s to work as a commercial traveller for Thomas Ibbotson but had soon entered into a partnership with one Henry Johnson so as to do business in his own right. In 1837, they had built a new steel works on Savile Street and the company grew rapidly, becoming a publicly quoted company in 1865. Some years later, they entered the shipbuilding field by acquiring the Birkenhead yards of Laird Brothers, the company then becoming known as Cammell Laird. Years of experience in manufacturing armour plate saw them, in 1894, joining an international syndicate to control prices and divide up the orders. Other members of this exclusive world club of armour manufacturers included: Vickers, John Brown, Dillinger – Heuten, Krupps, Acieres de la Marine, Schneider, Chatillon, Bethlehem Steel and Carnegie.

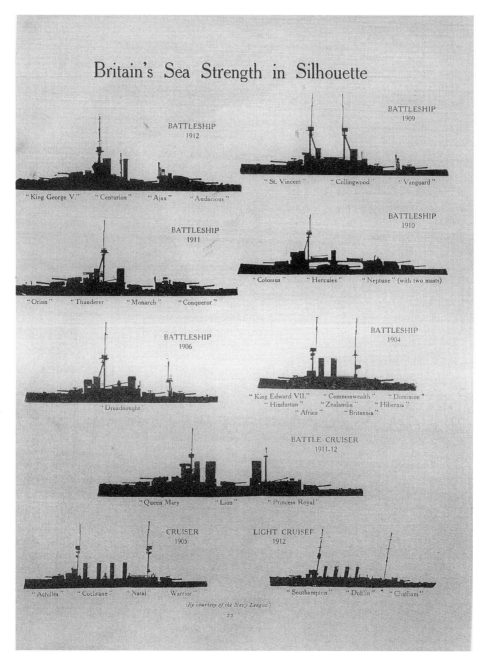

Key ships of the Royal Navy just prior to the outbreak of World War One.
(D.S. Dalton)

Shields for Carriage Garrison B. L. 6-inch and 9.2-inch Guns, Hadfield's Patent "Era" Cast Steel

Examples of Hadfield's cast armour quality gun shields. (Sheffield Libraries, Archives and Information, 623.4, with permission)

Trench mortars were made at a number of local engineering works. This example was manufactured by Hattersley and Davidson. (Sheffield Libraries, Archives and Information, S 10741, with permission)

In 1914, the Cyclops works was capable of producing 15,000 tons of armour plate annually, from 2 inches to the thickest then required by any of the naval constructors; 15,000 tons of axles as well as forgings, tool steels, files and rasps. Their Grimesthorpe Works was responsible for producing slabs for armour plate, forgings, marine ordnance castings and that oft forgotten, but vital component ... springs. They also had a plant at Penistone to the north of Sheffield that had been acquired in 1847. Here they had produced mainly railway components including fish-plates, railway tyres, axles and rails. Their labour force, excluding those employed in the Birkenhead shipyards, increased from 4,894 in 1914 to 7,256 in 1918.[2]

Cammell-Laird, which was also engaged in building warships at its Birkenhead shipyards, also undertook the building, and running of a shell factory at Nottingham. This factory, established under the 1915 Munitions of War Act, was situated in an area where a suitable pool of labour existed. The company refused to accept any government commission for this undertaking, which they managed in addition to their other manufacturing plants as well as their joint interests in the Coventry Ordnance Works.

John Brown was born in 1816 in Fargate in the centre of Sheffield and started his career, rather reluctantly, as an apprentice linen draper. He moved quickly to a firm of steel, cutlery and file manufacturers where he saw greater opportunities to develop his talents. In 1844 this ambitious and energetic young man set up his own steel manufacturing business in Orchard Street, on what is now the site of a shopping precinct. The business grew rapidly and by 1856 was operating from premises in Savile Street in the Don Valley where, in 1856 it took out a license to manufacture steel by the new Bessemer, pneumatic process. It was reluctant to start production, since other companies that had bought the license were achieving poor results. It would take Henry Bessemer himself to show the dubious Sheffield steel masters how successful the method could be if worked correctly. In 1861, John Brown's began melting steel successfully using the Bessemer method after being impressed by a trial at Bessemer's premises. In the years following its formation, John Brown's became a well-established arms manufacturer and in 1867, the company's founder was rewarded for his efforts with a knighthood.

From such relatively small beginnings John Brown's expanded not only its steelworks but had also gained control over its own iron mines and blast furnaces as well as a number of local collieries. These collieries, which included Rotherham Main, Aldwarke Main and

The humble file was required in tens of thousands. Workers at Cammel Laird are pictured making them. (Sheffield Libraries, Archives and Information, CL 338.4, with permission)

Carr House, employed more men than did the Atlas Works and by 1914 were producing, 2,500,000 tons of gas, steam and house coals annually.[3]

The company had also acquired a seventy-acre shipyard on the Clyde and had an interest in Belfast's Harland and Wolff shipyards as well as jointly owning the Coventry Ordnance Works. The company was able to build and equip warships with little involvement from other enterprises. Its armour plate mill was one of the largest in the world, capable of rolling plates up to forty-eight feet in length and up to 30 inches thick. Their heavy forge had made turbine drums for H.M.S. *Dreadnought, Inflexible, Indomitable, Indefatigable, Temeraire, Hercules, Bristol* and *Colossus* as well as those for over fifty destroyers.

Vickers, however, was by far the area's largest manufacturer. The company could trace its origins to the 1750s when Marshall's had established premises in the Millsands area of Sheffield. By the 1840s,

An empty shell machining shop at Cammel Laird just prior to the outbreak of World War One. (Sheffield Libraries, Archives and Information, CL 338.4, with permission)

Edward Vickers was able to gain control of the business, which continued operating as Naylor Vickers until 1867 when the limited company Vickers Sons and Co. was formed. In 1863, the highly profitable and expansive company decided to move to more spacious accommodation. It acquired land in the lower Don Valley from Lord Fitzwilliam and began building the new River Don Works. Only a slump in the early 1880s caused it to enter the armaments trade and by 1890, it had manufactured its first armour plate and artillery piece. From an estimated value of £17,335 in 1837, the company grew into one, which, in 1918, was only bettered by Coats, Lever Bros. and Imperial Tobacco in terms of its capital. Vickers had become a global organisation with a manufacturing network stretching as far as Japan, Russia, Spain and Italy.

Vickers' manufacturing activities embraced not only steel production, but also shipbuilding, aircraft and ordnance production. In 1901, this integration had enabled it to complete H.M.S. V*engeance*, the first ship in the Royal Navy to be built, powered, armoured and armed by one supplier. Vickers' expansionist strategy

A large slotting machine engaged in trimming armour plate. This example was sited at John Brown's Atlas works. (Sheffield Libraries, Archives and Information, JB 338.4, with permission)

had led to the acquisition of Barrow's Naval Construction and Armament Company in 1897 as well as that of Maxim Nordenfeldt and at this point the company became known as Vickers Son and Maxim Ltd. This takeover was promptly followed by the purchase of the North Kent Ironworks together with its important shell works. These acquisitions enabled the group to manufacture a vast range of military hardware and, in 1902, it expanded again by acquiring 50% of the ordinary share capital of Wm. Beardmore & Co. This company, with its 12,000-ton press, had specialised in the manufacture of armour and had been rumoured to be contemplating competition with Vickers by entering the ordnance market in its own right. By 1911, the group's name had changed once again to that of Vickers Ltd.

Vickers had, for a number of years, been a very substantial naval contractor but received only small orders from the War Office. In the

STEAM HAMMER FOR FORGING PROJECTILES.

John Brown's steel and projectile manufacturing facility. Note the foreman in his bowler hat. (Sheffield Libraries, Archives and Information, JB 338.4, with permission)

HYDRAULIC PRESSES FOR MAKING SHELLS.

7th January, 1916.

Dear Sirs,

It is with very great pleasure that I take this opportunity, on behalf of the Board of Admiralty, of congratulating your firm on the manner in which by their efforts they have contributed so materially to the strength of the Royal Navy.

Without going into details of the work which you have completed, and the work which you have well in hand at the present time, I hope you will allow me to express the warm appreciation of the Board of Admiralty of the excellent management and of the whole-hearted and devoted co-operation of your employees generally which have combined to produce these satisfactory results.

Messrs.John Brown & Company.

(Sheffield Libraries, Archives and Information, JB 338.4, with permission)

years 1910–1914, War Office orders only averaged some £ 55,000 per annum, including those for eleven machine guns, whilst Admiralty contracts for the same period averaged £3million overall. The war changed that as the company soon became a player in the War Office's attempts to fulfill its ever-growing requirements. As the conflict grew the Army's shortcomings, particularly in terms of heavy artillery, became acute and Vickers rose to meet the crisis, eventually becoming, jointly with Armstrong's, the War Office's major supplier of artillery, especially for 18 pounder, 6-inch and 9.2-inch siege howitzers.

One of the first test firings of the Maxim machine-gun at Vickers. (Sheffield Libraries, Archives and Information, S 10873, with permission)

At the height of the war it employed over 16,000 workers at its River Don Works.

Even the city's smaller companies added to the area's growing contribution to the supremacy of wartime production. Samuel Osborn's was engaged in manufacturing drills, tool steels, milling cutters, sheets, springs, castings and files; none of which had obvious military uses but without them, the war machine could never have been created or maintained. Its foundry produced castings for more obviously military related products including, sea mines, depth charge throwers and bomb cases as well as tank components. They also rolled 11/14% manganese sheet steel which, when pressed into the ubiquitous "tin hat" worn by the British soldier from 1916 onwards, was destined to become such a recurring image of the First World War.

A number of steel works in the Sheffield area had been amongst the pioneers in developing high-grade tool and high-speed steels, using combinations of the alloying elements of tungsten, chromium and molybdenum. These very specialised materials had been developed to increase productivity in the machining of metals and as

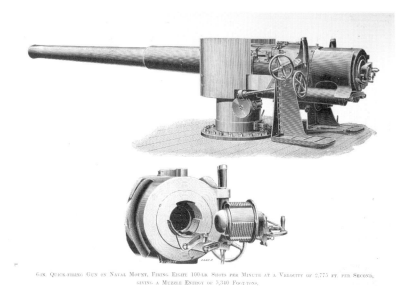

6-IN. QUICK-FIRING GUN ON NAVAL MOUNT, FIRING EIGHT 100-LB. SHOTS PER MINUTE AT A VELOCITY OF 2,775 FT. PER SECOND, GIVING A MUZZLE ENERGY OF 3,310 FOOT-TONS.

6-inch quickfiring gun on naval mount manufactured by Vickers Sons and Maxim. (Sheffield Libraries, Archives and Information, 338 SQ, with permission)

60-IN. LATHE. TURNING EXTERIOR OF GUN.

A 13.5-inch naval gun weighing 67 tons being machined at the River Don works of Vickers Sons and Maxim. (Sheffield Libraries, Archives and Information, 338, with permission)

a result, they had become an essential requirement in almost all engineering activities. Consequently, they were in high demand, both nationally and internationally. The requirement for tool steels rapidly

ARMOURED HOOD.

An armour quality cast steel hood for a Dreadnought cast at the River Don works of Vickers Sons and Maxim. (Sheffield Libraries, Archives and Information, with permission)

Plan of the River Don works of Vickers Sons and Maxim c. 1910. (Sheffield Libraries, Archives and Information, with permission)

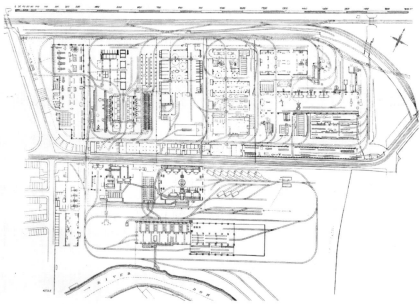

PLAN OF THE RIVER DON WORKS.

made their manufacture one of Sheffield's busiest steel making sectors. Amongst the manufacturers of these steels were Samuel Osborn, Edgar Allen, J Beardshaw, Marsh Brothers, William Jessop, Seebohm – Dieckstahl, (which would change its name to the more anglicised Arthur Balfour & Co. as anti- German feelings grew) Kayser Ellison's (which did not!), Spear & Jackson and Thos. Andrews. Output of high speed steels more than trebled during the course of the conflict, reaching more than 18,000 tons annually, but even so Sheffield's manufacturers could not keep pace with the demand which included export orders from Canada, France, Italy, Russia and one of over 3,000 tons from the Japanese Arsenal. So great was this demand that many manufacturers were a year or more behind schedule.

The high numbers of shrapnel wounds to the head brought about the recognition of a need for some form of protective headwear. The War Office agreed and a suitable design was quickly approved for issue to the troops in the trenches. The specified material to be used for these "tin" helmets was Sir Robert Hadfield's 11/14% manganese steel which was tough, durable, abrasion resistant and non-magnetic. Supplies of steel slabs were readily available from both Hadfield's and Edgar Allen. In early 1916, the twenty sheet mills in the Sheffield area were asked to complete one million blanks…. in a hurry. These were for the first batch of helmets to be issued to troops taking part in the major offensive of that year on the Somme.

Rotherham's many steel and engineering works were just as busy as those in Sheffield and were suffering the same problems. Coaxing as much production out of their plants, whilst at the same time working within a limited supply of labour, was an endless problem for them all. During the four years of war, Park Gate Iron and Steel produced over 425,500 tons of finished steel. This was widely used for manufacturing shells, for shipbuilding, for use on the railways and for all manner of civilian and military uses. In 1916, in order to try and meet the ever-increasing demand for steel, a third blast furnace was added and women workers were introduced into the steelworks for the first time. These women were used to fill many of the jobs which had been vacated when 362 male employees had joined the forces. Thirty-two of these men, were destined to be killed on active service.

John Baker's of Kilnhurst had been primarily engaged in manufacturing railway axles and wheels but in 1915, as a direct result of the shell shortage, it adapted all of its hydraulic presses to the job of shell making. At the end of the war, it had produced 6 million

Hadfield's extol the virtues of their steel helmet. (Sheffield Libraries, Archives and Information with permission)

shells, some of which had been made by weekend "scratch" teams of local worthies who voluntarily put their hands to doing their bit for the war effort.

The Steel, Peech and Tozer steel works was so deeply involved in melting and rolling shell steels, amongst others, that during the course of the war, a completely new works was built on a green field site at Templeborough to help alleviate the shortage of steel affecting all metal working industries. This new works, comprising of open-hearth steel melting furnaces and rolling mills, was built over the site of a Roman fort and complemented the existing plants. These other works, consisting of melting shops, rolling mills, forges and machine shops, worked on shifts throughout the conflict and produced gun barrels, shells and a range of other military requirements.

Chapter Three

Problems and Scandals

The Liberal government of Prime Minister Asquith firmly embraced the principles of *laissez faire* and for many of its members war was contrary to their basic beliefs. Nonetheless, the war was a grim reality that had to be faced but it was a reality, which, it was hoped, would disturb normal life for the briefest time possible. Despite prophetic predictions to the contrary from some quarters, it was almost universally expected that the war would be over quickly. Government controls, not to mention conscription, were concepts which flew in the face of the policy of "business as usual" and the popular belief that the war might be "over by Christmas", saw young men in their thousands flocking to the join the colours before it ended. Meanwhile, the small, well-trained British Expeditionary Force (BEF) had sailed for the continent and had taken their place alongside the French armies on the fields of Belgium. The British Army, like the armies of all combatant nations, was not ready for what was about to unfold. Its standard allocation of machine-guns was two per battalion – roughly the same figure per battalion for the German Army in 1914, given its greater size – with very few on order. In artillery, the BEF was deficient. The British Army's experience in the relatively small conflicts of the latter part of the nineteenth century had led to a reliance on field artillery, particularly the 18-pounder gun, firing shrapnel shells. It therefore lacked sufficient numbers of the heavy guns and shells required to destroy the deep dugouts and wire obstacles so characteristic of the trench warfare that would dominate operations in almost every theatre.

The small British Army had, initially, been involved in battles around Mons and Le Cateau in late August 1914 in an attempt to stem the German advance on Paris, after which it began an exhausting retreat towards the French capital. The retreat continued until 5th September when, on the line of the River Marne, it took part with the French in a successful counter attack, which drove the Germans back to the River Aisne where both sides dug in. By mid October the BEF had become embroiled in the bloody battles around the Belgian town of Ypres, (now marked as Ieper on modern day maps). Casualties were very high and by Christmas 1914, some

80,000 men out of its establishment of 160,000 had become casualties; 30,000 of that figure being killed during the First Battle of Ypres alone.

Britain had few reserves of either men or munitions but such were the losses that generals began demanding more of everything from home. A policy of industrial and economic *laissez faire* would prove incompatible with the demands, which the war was making on the nation.

The situation created by these very urgent, but unplanned, requirements for weapons saw the private armaments companies trying to deal with panic ordering as well as with growing shortages of both men and materials. Vickers reported that on 25th August 1914 it was asked to deliver 78, 18 pounder guns no later than the beginning of October. This contract was then increased to 360 for delivery by August 1915. Another example of panic ordering was a contract drawn up on 4th September 1914, for Vickers to produce and deliver sixteen 9.2-inch siege howitzers. This figure was subsequently revised upwards to 32, for delivery no later than August 1915. Vickers was then asked to respond to an urgent appeal by designing a new 6-inch howitzer and received orders for four of them ... swiftly increased by another twelve. These were the first of the many thousands Vickers and other manufacturers would produce. The type of warfare, which was developing in France – trench warfare – required specialised weapons and unlike the Germans, who had learned some of the lessons from the American Civil War and more recently the Russo – Japanese War, the British Army lacked trench artillery. Vickers was able to meet this challenge by designing and manufacturing a trench howitzer. In June 1915, 127 of these weapons were in service together with adequate supplies of ammunition.

General Sir Douglas Haig had, before the outbreak of hostilities, once declared the machine-gun to be an "overrated weapon". Its effects upon infantry on the battlefield soon showed it to be one of the effective weapons in what had effectively become a war of siege. The Vickers model, a development of the older Maxim weapon, which had been made by the Vickers Maxim Company, was initially produced at its Erith, Kent works. In the first eight weeks of the war, Vickers received orders for 1,792 guns. Initially, only 192 had been ordered and in September an additional 100 were on order. In less than three weeks a further 1,000 were ordered, followed a week later by a request for an extra 500. In the following month the French Government added to the chaotic production and delivery situation by ordering the gun to be supplied at a rate of fifty per week! This demand, quite simply, could not be met by undirected industry – private or not – and actual deliveries revealed the desperate situation. The War Office ordered 2,338 new model 18 pounder guns. These were scheduled to be ready for service by July 1915. In fact, only 1,096 were available on time. As for the Vickers machine-gun orders, only 1,022 were actually delivered by July 1915. An army, which, in the past, had neither relied on modern infantry weapons nor upon heavy artillery had to make rapid strides in rectifying its weaknesses and the strain was beginning to tell.

As difficult as the situation was with the supply of guns, so too was the supply of shells. A gun is just so much useless metal without an adequate supply of ammunition. In the first weeks of the war the private arms manufacturers received large orders, many of them for shrapnel. This anti-personnel projectile had been extremely useful during the Boer War, but proved to be less so against the heavily entrenched Germans and had limited capability in destroying barbed wire entanglements. Not only were the initial orders placed for the wrong type of shell but the War Office added to the armaments companies' difficulties by expecting them, out of patriotism alone, to cope with orders for some six and a quarter million shells. Meanwhile, out of all the Government's own ordnance factories, contracts had only been placed to supply 812,000 shells. Labour shortages, compounded by the War Office's insistence on changing priorities and of increasing the rate of production (on 10 November 1914 it asked for 35,000 shells per week ... four days later it was asking for 55,000 per week) left the manufacturers in a state of alarm, particularly since the drain of labour into the forces went on unabated.

In the first few months of the war, the River Don Works lost 1,000 skilled young men who left their jobs to enlist. As early as December 1914, Vickers was lobbying the Government to train women for work in the shell shops. The initial impact of the war on many working women was in terms of job losses, especially those employed in domestic service. Many now sought war work and began to vocalise their desire. Munitions work was not, in reality, a highly skilled job, nor did it require the armaments firms, who were specialised engineers, to mass-produce the large quantities of shells being consumed in the fighting. Prophetically, Vickers was already asking for some form of central direction of labour into the factories and for recruiting officers to steer clear of certain specified occupations and especially its own workers.

Certain sectors of society considered that the problems of supply were being exacerbated by the rise in earnings that full employment and overtime had created. Workers who, in the recent past, had suffered the vagaries of slumps, unemployment and low wages, now found that the iron law of supply and demand was working in their favour. Much of this new found spending power, it was claimed, was being spent on the "demon drink" and, as a result, drunkenness in the labour force was causing war production to suffer.

Both the Admiralty and the War Office were equally aware of the deleterious effects of excessive drinking and as a consequence, one of the earliest orders under the 1914 Defence of the Realm Act was one which stated: *The competent naval or military authority may, by order, require all premises licensed for the sale of intoxicating liquor within or in the neighbourhood of any defended harbour to be closed except during such hours as may be specified by the order.*[1]

Other restrictions were imposed under the Intoxicating Liquor (Temporary Restriction) Act of 31 August 1914, which gave the Chief Officer of Police or the licensing justices power to impose restrictions upon the sale of alcohol. By the close of 1914, nearly half of the one thousand licensing authorities in England and Wales had used the Act to restrict opening hours and those in Sheffield had been especially diligent. Heavy drinking, which had historically been a necessary part of industrial working life and culture was, as a result, being reduced by these measures.

The Chancellor of the Exchequer, David Lloyd George, was nevertheless dissatisfied even with these measures. "The lure of drink" seemed, to him, to be the root of the munitions problem. "Drink", he claimed, "is doing us more damage in the war than all the German submarines put together".[2] A month later, on 29th March 1915 he added, "We are fighting Germany, Austria and Drink and, as far as I can see the greatest of these deadly foes is Drink"[3] The infantryman in the trenches must have felt very puzzled to learn that a pint of beer was more deadly than the trench bomb that had just exploded in his vicinity!

A moral crusade led by Lord Kitchener and supported by the King, called for abstinence and for even tighter controls to be introduced. A government sponsored report into bad time keeping in shipbuilding, transport and munitions, presented on 29th April 1915, concluded that, " the main reasons for the loss of time was the ease with which men now enjoying high rates of wages and abundance of employment could obtain beer and spirits".[4] The report made no mention of those other classes in society who were untroubled by the need to restrict consumption in the name of the war effort, nor of the working conditions many workers suffered.

The Adelphi Hotel, Market Street. Just one of Sheffield's many working class public houses. (Sheffield Libraries, Archives and Information, S 06904, with permission)

Whether drink was a factor or not, British industry, as undirected as it was, still could not meet War Office requirements. By May 1915 only about a third of the six million shells, which should have been delivered, had actually been supplied. Even Lord Kitchener, that great driving force who had brow beaten the armaments manufacturers into accepting these orders, had to admit they were, "far in excess of the capacity to produce".[5] The truth, as ever, was an amalgam of many factors. The War Office were often inept and unrealistic but labour was rejoicing in its new found wealth and using market forces in trying to secure their position by obstructing the use of "dilutee" labour. The manufacturers, similarly, were celebrating their increased profits. The war, which had been predicted would be short lived, was developing into one of long-term commitment both militarily, and industrially. Neither the military nor industry, initially, was prepared for the long struggle and it would be the industrialists, and more specifically the workers, who would be the first to receive public criticism.

Yet work in the factories was not easy and never had been. It was usually heavy and demanding, often in unpleasant conditions coupled with long working hours and frequently poor wages. Many of the new munitions workers found the change in life to be a great shock. Arthur Bennett complained of being, "mightily sick of the whole business". His first wages amounted to £ I-2-0d for a week of thirteen hour shifts. By January 1916 though, with his improving manual skills, his weekly piecework for 1,494 shells earned him nearly £ 4-3-0d. Despite the reward of these relatively high wages he found the night shifts to be "difficult" and like many before, and since, considered that the "man who invented it ought to be shot". Shift work had been an established feature of working life for many of Sheffield and District's workers for years and like most, Arthur Bennett loathed them. "Working in false light with a rotten atmosphere and sleeping whilst the sun shines is as fatal to the strongest constitution, as it would be to a flower under similar circumstances."[6] Family life for a shift-working man was usually difficult if non-existent. Mothers had to keep children quiet whilst their fathers slept and any family discussions, generally, had to wait until the week's work was over. Even then many men would take themselves, "off to the pub", to relax with other men.

Despite patriotic calls for production, industrial unrest was growing and would continue to do so throughout the war. The dilution of labour, the rising cost of living and the real effects of the restrictions of the Munitions of War Act on a worker's ability to change jobs, all added to unrest. Perhaps the most potent contribution to unrest, however, was the workers' widely held belief that the industrialists and company owners were guilty of war profiteering.

In May 1915, the effects of Britain's industrial shortcomings on the military campaign in France and Flanders came to a head. The BEF had fought its first major battle in its own right at Neuve Chappelle two months earlier and followed this up with an attack on the strategically important Aubers Ridge in Artois on May 9th, in concert with the French. As in the BEF's previous battle at Neuve Chappelle there was to be a preliminary artillery bombardment, which was expected to breach the German barbed wire entanglements on two specific sectors and destroy the trench system along with key strong points. This was then to be followed by a massed infantry attack upon the German lines. It was hoped that this assault would find the defenders in a state of disarray following the artillery's earlier attentions, but when the attack went in all too often the attacking forces were met by unobstructed machine-gun fire that cut them down in their thousands.

The initial British bombardment at Aubers Ridge was not only inadequate but also poorly planned by the staff officers. Few of the shells were high explosive, the rest were of shrapnel, which had little effect upon wire or on well-entrenched humanity. Even this poor mixture of ammunition was doubly damned since there were neither sufficient shells nor guns to produce more than a thirty-minute artillery preparation of the German lines. In addition many of the heavier guns were old and worn and some were already obsolete, which greatly affected their accuracy. Prior to the outbreak of war the British had been slower than either the Germans or the French to respond to the scale of munitions supply required for this type of warfare. Typically, the French had thirty-five guns per mile of front whilst the British, at that time, could manage only nineteen of all types. The battle of Aubers Ridge turned out to be a dismal failure. Heavy losses were incurred and there was much heated debate about where the blame for the failure should lie. The British generals needed scapegoats.

Some politicians in Britain were unhappy with a style of government which reacted to events rather than anticipated them. The Conservatives, in particular, wanted firmer action, and it was hardly surprising that this latest military failure should be brought to the attention of the press. Hitherto, strict censorship had prevailed but the British Commander in Chief, Field Marshal Sir John French, decided to let *The Times* have information concerning the failure of those at home to supply his army with sufficient munitions and of the high proportion of shells that failed to explode.

The general outcry, following these revelations, within parliament and the media, brought about the creation of Coalition Government. This administration now contained eight Conservatives but, most importantly, led to a change in Lloyd George's role from that of populist Chancellor, who claimed he could deal with the unions, to that of Minister of Munitions with very wide powers. Industry would now, at last, be controlled, labour directed and agreements reached about the future of "dilutee" labour. The sale of alcohol was to be even more restricted; young women would be directed into factories to make shells, often in new, purpose-built establishments. Industry's profits were to be controlled; strikes in all industries covered by the Munitions Act were to be prohibited; priorities were to be decided upon between the conflicting interests of the War Office and the Admiralty and conscription was to be introduced. Britain was now at total war with the government beginning to control more and more aspects of civilian life and individual freedom.

The newly created Ministry of Munitions undoubtedly benefited from earlier expansion plans, which were only just bearing fruit. The national output of shells soared; monthly output between May and July doubled from 200,000 to 400,000 pieces.[7]

Locally, Hadfield's, Firth's, Vickers and Cammell-Laird played key roles in the success of the new production organizations and groupings created by the Ministry. Firth's "mothered" the Halifax, Sheffield and Rotherham production groups, whilst Vickers carried out a similar role in the Birmingham area. Cammell-Laird, which was anxious to meet Ministry requirements, found neither sufficient space nor labour in Sheffield and so built and ran a new munitions factory in Nottingham. Hadfield's, finding sufficient space, built a new shell factory within its own works and, by the end of the war, was destined to become the City's biggest employer.

In December, Lloyd George was able to tell the House of Commons that there was, "no shortage of shells" and that, "… guns of all kinds, including big guns were coming forward in good numbers; machine-gun production in December was up five times over what it had been in June."[8]

Sheffield had its own wartime scandals, largely caused as a result of widespread hysteria and xenophobia. Official and popular hostility to the German community in Britain had quickly led to a policy of, and legislation for, the internment and repatriation of enemy nationals. This legislation affected all male citizens of military age of enemy countries, irrespective of rank. The four hundred or so members of Sheffield's German community, largely made up of pork butchers, engineers, managers, teachers, clerks, tailors and commercial travellers, were ordered to report to the city's central police station. Those who were included under the order were detained there for two nights before being sent, under escort, to York. From there, they went south to ships moored at Southend, before being transferred to the aliens' camp in Alexandra Palace, London. For some that wasn't the end of their travels. A now unknown number were taken to the large internment camp at Knockaloe on the Isle of Man. All were forcibly repatriated to Germany in 1919, including Julius Freund, Professor of German at the University of Sheffield. In 1921 there were only 176 German born citizens of Sheffield remaining in the city.

Despite internment, those who were excluded from the order still suffered from anti-German anger and suspicion that, occasionally,

Born a German, Antoine Droitcourt was working on an engineering contract at the outbreak of war and was interned. Documentary proof of his French parentage eventually helped to secure his release in 1916. (D.S. Dalton)

erupted in violence. Mobs in Sheffield and Rotherham attacked the retail premises of A. G. Friederich, Herman Zeiher and George Haimeman amongst others. Even the English were not immune. One, a Mr Leech, had his premises stoned, as his wife was German. To avoid these repercussions the firm of Seebohm and Dieckstahl, rather pragmatically, changed its name to that of its principal shareholder, Arthur Balfour but other companies were less fortunate. The Poldi Steelworks were wound up as an "alien business" as were

The disgraced Sheffield industrialist (Sir) Joseph Jonas. (Sheffield Libraries, Archives and Information, S 08117, with permission)

those of the Austro-German, Bohler Brothers with a branch in the city.

Sheffield's three notable, native German steelmakers, Charles Kayser, Paul Kuehnrich and Sir Joseph Jonas were all vulnerable, yet all managed, due to their ages, to avoid internment. Nevertheless, Sheffield's important Germans did not entirely escape the attentions of the authorities. Kuehnrich was accused of being a friend of the Kaiser; of having a secret army that he drilled at his residence in Ecclesall and of stockpiling arms and ammunition. Despite offers to allow the police to search his residence, he was continually hounded, being brought before the courts and twice fined. His first 'misdemeanour' was displaying a bright light outside his residence and his second the stockpiling of sixty-nine lbs of bacon!

The most serious case, even meriting national press coverage, was that of Sir Joseph Jonas who had been Lord Mayor of Sheffield in 1905. His 'crime' had, in fact, taken place before the war when, in 1913, he had allegedly passed on commercial information to Berlin. In 1918 he and two others, were charged with contravening the provisions of the Official Secrets Act, by communicating information of military value to an enemy. The trial took place at London's Central Criminal Courts. He was found not guilty of the original charge but guilty of the lesser count of misdemeanor, fined and censured. He is one of a small number to suffer the disgrace of having a knighthood revoked and he died less than three years later.

Chapter Four

Air Raids

The Royal Naval Air Service (R.N.A.S.), with the urging and backing of Winston Churchill, had begun air raids on the Germans in October 1914. A small force of canvas and wooden aircraft, operating from the Belgian coast, raided Zeppelin sheds dropping bombs on both Dusseldorf and Cologne. It is little wonder then that the Germans retaliated. Their airship raids across the British mainland, beginning in 1915, caused only relatively small amounts of damage by later standards but the psychological effects were considerable. Nowhere in the country was now safe from enemy action. Britain's civilian population and its industry were now being attacked at home. Following highly disruptive raids on other parts of England, Sheffield, with its high concentration of steel and armaments manufacturers, felt that it must be on the list of targets. Accordingly, the local authority produced civil defence instructions for such an eventuality.

Warnings of the presence of enemy aircraft within reach of the city were given on no less than twenty-three occasions in a period of just over three years. The first alarm was raised on 16th June 1915 with four more alarms being raised that year. In 1916, there were twelve alarms. In 1917, the alarms were only sounded on three occasions and, in the final year of the war, they were again sounded three times. Each time the alarm was raised the presumed target was Sheffield. Even without dropping a single bomb on their target, the fear and disruption caused by merely flying down wind, could be counted a success for the German Naval Air Division, which was responsible for most of Germany's aerial activity over the British mainland.

It has been estimated that the threat of aerial bombardment resulted in 17,341 officers and men being specifically retained in Great Britain for home anti-aircraft defence. Additionally, twelve Royal Flying Corps (R.F.C.) squadrons, comprising some 2,110 officers and men as well as 110 aeroplanes were also detailed for Home Defence duties. Sheffield had two landing sites at Redmires and Coal Aston, with a detachment of the R.N.A.S. stationed there as well as 'A' flight of 33 Squadron, the R.F.C., tasked for nocturnal sorties. The 12,000 men allocated to the nation's anti-aircraft guns could have found duties in the trenches.

The Royal Naval Air Service detachment (and mascots) based at Coal Aston.
(Sheffield Libraries, Archives and Information, S 09387, with permission)

Searchlights had also been provided and these were intended to play over the city in the search for the intruders. When operated they created much amusement for the younger element of the population. Given the general inability to train the lights onto the target accurately, they were more a symbol of defiance than of any real use in finding the elusive night-time raiders.

Meanwhile, learning from the experience of other major towns and cities, the Sheffield City Police Force prepared the populace for the expected onslaught by issuing detailed air raid precautions on 7th February 1916.

In order to defend the important industrial sites, anti-aircraft batteries had been situated at Wincobank Hill, The Manor and Ecclesall and instructions had been issued as to how to deal with any downed aircraft. In anticipation of heavy civilian casualties a detachment of the R.A.M.C. were stationed from 1915 at Hillsborough Barracks.

Additionally, each of Sheffield's eleven police stations was given an allocation of twenty N.C.Os and men. In the event of a raid, permission was granted for those men not required for ambulance duties to help the police in their duties.

Motorised ambulances were something of a novelty at the time but a number were obtained, frequently by private donation. Three ambulances, numbered 3, 5 and 34 owned by Sir Joseph Jonas, W. Drew and Wm.Cooke and Co. were allocated to police stations in Brightside. Other companies placed their vehicles around the city. It was a case, perhaps, of the named firms showing that they could respond to the nation's call in its hour of need.

The nation saw enemy spies everywhere and a spy phobia was prevalent as was the awareness that potential enemy agents could assist aerial raiders to their targets. Consequently, in the event of an air raid, instructions were given to seal off the city and ensure all lights were extinguished as well as checking on any traffic movements.[1] With reference to the city's steelworks an agreement was reached with the major producers and guidelines were laid down which, it was hoped, would reduce light emissions from the city's many furnaces. It was agreed that:

1) all outside lights were to be turned off.
2) all furnace doors were to be closed unless screened.
3) no steel casting or steel pouring from a furnace to take place unless the operation could be carried out within five minutes of the initial air raid warning being given, unless effectively screened from emitting light.
4) the blast to be shut off from all furnaces to prevent the emission of light.
5) no ladles containing hot metal to be left in the open.

These provisions, naturally, had the effect of reducing output. They also added to the realisation that this was now a war where the Home Front was just as much under attack as anywhere else.

The 1915 Zeppelin raids on parts of the British mainland caused much consternation, if not panic, within both the general population and in military circles called upon to counter the threat. Steps had been taken to improve anti-aircraft defences as well as developing more effective, mixed explosive and incendiary bullets with which to arm the intercepting aircraft of the R.F.C. Needless to say, the Germans reacted to these measures by improving the efficiency and flight characteristics of their lighter than air craft.

By 1916, a new range of highflying super Zeppelin had been developed each costing, at the time, DM 2,800,000. By any standards, they were gigantic creations. Each was powered by six 240 h.p. Maybach engines and had a crew of 17. They could reach over 64 m.p.h. and cruise at an altitude of 3,900 metres and sometimes even higher; beyond the effective range of artillery when they had disposed of their bomb load. With a length of 198 metres, they could carry five thousand kgs of high explosives and incendiary bombs. They weighed 31,400 kgs unladen and could carry 6,250 kgs of fuel, giving them a range of some 7,400 km. On the night of 25th/26th September 1916, Sheffield was the target planned for one of these flying monsters.[2]

When the alarm was raised, all traffic in the city was brought to a halt; people were urged to return home or to seek safe shelter and cigarette and pipe smoking was forbidden. On hearing the alarms, however, large numbers of the local civilian population became very excitable and the police were, eventually, forced to open public parks to ease the congestion in the streets. Here many thousands of more or less terrified, hysterical men, women and children congregated to see the excitement or perhaps await their fate. Others ran in panic into nearby woods and fields and many cringed, fearfully, in their homes. At about 11p.m. the Zeppelin approached Sheffield from the east. It passed unmolested over the city and apparently went away only to return some time later. Its engines, according to one local, Henry Tatton, on Matilda Street, "sounded like those of a traction engine". The machine appeared to him to be approaching from the direction of Darnall and going toward Woodseats and Crookes.

The first bomb fell at 12.20 a.m., some one and a half hours after the raising of the initial alarm. Henry Tatton said there were, "bright flashes of blue light and sharp, very loud reports, coming from the direction of the Midland Station". In fact, the first bomb had dropped at the corner of Burngreave Cemetery and during the fifteen minutes of the raid, thirty-six bombs were dropped, comprising eighteen incendiaries and a similar number of high explosives. All fell in a line toward Washford Bridge. Eighty-nine houses, one hotel and one chapel were destroyed or seriously damaged; a further one hundred and fifty houses were less seriously damaged.

Loud explosions had shattered the peace of an autumn night, waking many who had not heard the air raid alarm. Five hysterical, women woke Arthur Bennett who, having been on his day shift, was then in bed in his lodgings. He calmed them down, aware that their part of the city had, fortunately, escaped attack. Later he wrote that the shock of the bombing to Sheffield was tremendous and that Sheffield's escape from serious damage had been nothing short of miraculous.

A local newspaper report, written on 4th December 1918, after the strict wartime censorship rules had been relaxed, claimed that the incendiaries caused at most £426 worth of damage, with the high explosive weapons being responsible for the majority of the damage and for all the fatalities. The Tyler family of 146, Corby Street, numbering seven in all, was wiped out. A similar fate befell the members of the Hames, Rhodes, Harrison, Newton and Southerington families, who were all sheltering at 10 Cossey Street when it was hit. Twenty-eight people lost their lives that night. The youngest victim was 2 year-old John Tyler, the oldest 76 year-old Ann Coogan of Petre Street. Most of the victims were buried in Burngreave Cemetery at what was described in the local paper as a "moving service". Sheffield's vital wartime production was not apparently affected by this attack.

The Zeppelin raid on Sheffield caused the first military damage in the area since the Civil War. Here, police and soldiers search for survivors on Cossey Street, Darnall. (Sheffield Libraries, Archives and Information, S 02359, with permission)

Yet, why did no one on the gun sites see the raiders? Where were the searchlights and more importantly, why did none of Sheffield's three anti-aircraft batteries open fire at the intruders? The official press view, written many months after the event was that, "to have illuminated the sky with searchlights would have merely guided the intruders on their erratic trip across the city and that they were at too high an altitude to be effectively reached".

However, could it be that military discipline had slipped? A contemporary record, written by Henry Tatton, whose habit was to record tit bits of news, claimed that not a shot was fired at the Zeppelin since all the batteries' officers, who presumably were required to be present in order to open fire, were at a ball in the Grand Hotel.[3]

The raid lived on in folk memory for countless years but is now all but forgotten. In truth, it was, by the standards of the Second World War, a minor affair but those potent and terrifying memories of Sheffield's first air raid lived on amongst the generation of 1914-18. No longer were wars to be fought solely within the confines of a battlefield. Future wars would involve civilians as a matter of course. Civilian terror and the disruption of the means to wage war would become a justifiable feature of future wars. Henceforth, for some, pacifism and appeasement would become a duty.

Chapter Five

A Fit Country for Heroes

In an attempt to try and give some moral justification for the war, it was said frequently that it was being fought so as to "end all wars". This proved to be a false expectation but the horrors of total war and more particularly the horrors of trench warfare needed some form of justification. The war still needed winning and, despite false hopes and failures, the battles of July and August 1918, saw the Allies gaining the ascendancy. War weariness was widespread but there now existed a real prospect of ending the conflict. The Armistice, when it came on 11th November 1918, saw the Allies counting not only the dreadful human cost, but also the economic price the war had incurred.

In over four years of war, steel production had increased across the board by 25%, as a result of emergency measures. Investments in new

Peace celebrations on Summer Street. November 1918. (Sheffield Libraries, Archives and Information, S 00145, with permission)

plant and equipment had been considerable. Cammell-Laird had installed six new open hearth furnaces and a new cogging mill at its Penistone works, whilst in Rotherham's Templeborough area, Steel Peech and Tozer, Samuel Fox and Appleby Frodingham had jointly built a new steel works with a melting plant designed to use scrap and domestic, cold pig iron. These three companies, together with the Workington Iron and Steel Company, would merge to form the giant United Steel Companies with government backing, the forerunner of similar post war combinations. Others like the small steel companies of Marsh Bros. and Brittain's also found that the peacetime logic, out of wartime co-operation, would be to amalgamate. Ironically, Sheffield's middle sized producers, Edgar Allen, Samuel Osborn and Arthur Balfour, were mooting the possibility of amalgamation as early as 1918 but it would take another half century and more for these rationalisations to happen and by then, arguably, it was too late to save the city's basic industry. The ending of the war offered the daunting prospects of excess capacity in a world which would soon need much less steel, but war had been the spur in the creation of new methods and materials and in these the city's industrialists considered themselves well placed for the future.

A Mk IV tank of World War One. Tanks were to revolutionise warfare after their first use at Flers on the Somme in September 1916. (D.S. Dalton)

Wartime military developments saw the infantry tank introduced as a revolutionary battle-winning machine and whilst none were manufactured in Sheffield, their armour plating had all been rolled, machined and heat-treated by the city's specialist armour producers. Naval guns and battleships had grown in size; submarine warfare had matured sufficiently to raise the spectre of effective naval blockades, even for a nation inadequately equipped with surface vessels. The most remarkable developments though had been within the field of military aviation.

The primitive, heavier than air machines of 1914 had, in the cauldron of war, developed at an extraordinary rate and now offered military strategists the possibilities of extending warfare into civilian and industrial centres. This possibility was further fostered in the 1920s and 30s by the widely held belief that the bomber would always get through. Warfare had encouraged manufacturers to develop more reliable engines and airframes that were both lighter and stronger. Peace now offered the prospect of developing civil aviation, long distance flight already being a reality. The future development of the internal combustion engine, which also powered the vehicles replacing horse drawn transport, was also vital to the progress of aviation. Sheffield was at the forefront of metallurgical research and had developed not only the steels but also the heat treatment techniques that reliable engine components needed. One significant development, which came as a result of research prior to and during the war into the erosion of rifle and gun barrels, was the discovery, by Harry Brearley, of stainless steels. These steels would have a profound effect for heat and corrosion resisting applications in general but the future development of aviation would come to rely heavily upon Harry Brearley's discovery.

The world, Europe in particular, would never be the same but the government's goal was to return to pre-war economic conditions as quickly as possible. Lloyd George wanted to get the soldiers home and to ensure they received fair treatment. In the event, the adoption of long-winded demobilisation processes led to considerable protest on the part of the troops with many feeling bitter at what they saw as shoddy treatment. Punishment for the Kaiser, making Germany pay and better social conditions for the people of Britain were further aims of the government. Social improvements depended upon Britain regaining its economic position in world markets but after a short post war boom the economy went into a long period of decline. The steel industry was badly hit and worse still, with the general desire for disarmament and a government happy to make swingeing cuts in spending, Sheffield's armaments manufacturers were dealt a double blow.

Cyclical and seasonal unemployment were well known occurrences but the economic events of the 1920s and 30s were Britain's first experience of structural unemployment. Its causes were numerous; instability in the world financial markets; excess capacity, often in uncompetitive manufacturing plants which had expanded to meet wartime demands and the collapse of traditional export markets. These were just some of its causes but one major factor was the "cheap, real money" financial policies pursued by the governments of the day. The belief was that these policies would create conditions where things would return to normal. In reality they exacerbated the recession. By 1930, 2,071,900 insured workers, throughout the country were unemployed and the real figure was even higher if those workers who were unemployed but uninsured were included. This was scarcely a land fit for heroes to live in!

Sheffield's 1931 unemployment rate was running at 23.1%. This was higher than Glasgow (21.4%), Newcastle (20.8%), or indeed Liverpool (20.6%). Over half of Sheffield's steelworkers found themselves unemployed and annual benefit payments were running at £ 2,162,000, compared with the 1928 figure of £ 808,000. The city, which had relied for its prosperity upon its steel industry, was suffering. Amongst the measures adopted by the City Council to help alleviate some of the worst problems was the provision of free meals for the most deserving of its school children. In 1931 they provided 1,126,111 free school meals, sometimes to the extent of three meals a day. The Council also organised schemes to provide shoes and clothes to the most underprivileged of these pupils. These clothes were clearly identified by the Council, in an attempt to stop the unscrupulous pawning them.

The 'means test', which was administered by local Public Assistance Committees, endeavoured, at government insistence, to reduce the amount of benefit being paid to the unemployed and was a most hated and divisive measure. It was so despised that some local authorities refused to fully implement the regulations. Rotherham was one such local authority that found itself in receipt of the full wrath of the government and official nominees were appointed to run the scheme. The working class had seen their real incomes rise during the recent war, due to a demand for their labour, but they had made real sacrifices, not least of which were the numbers of young men who had been killed and maimed in their hundreds of thousands. The failed 1926 General Strike had left the unions in disarray.

Consequently, the heaviest of economic burdens were placed upon the poorest and least able members of society.

Despite its earlier role in contributing to an allied victory in the First World War, Sheffield's steel-works struggled throughout the years of recession and would not assume national importance until the country again became occupied with the urgent need to re-arm. By then, most of the old steel barons had departed the scene and a new breed of senior management had assumed control of the city's industry. Few were local men with any personal commitment toward the area. Sheffield's industrialists had seldom been generous, very few had been benefactors, none had built impressive headquarters as statements of their pride and as a consequence, unlike some Victorian cities, it lacked impressive buildings. The new owners were even less interested in the city's aesthetics but would be more than capable of managing the demands that re-armament brought.

One consequence of the First World War was that some local companies – Brown Bayley for example – had ceased being solely producers of semi-finished products ... billets and blooms for sale to

The 1930s saw major demolition work take place as redundant plant was removed. Here a large overhead crane is brought down at English Steel Corporation's works. (Sheffield Libraries, Archives and Information, S 09807, with permission)

re-rollers and forgers. This company had begun to manufacture in its own right as well as supplying other manufacturers with the steels they needed. It had joined the ranks of Sheffield companies which had developed a degree of vertical integration and whose metallurgical experience would be put to good use. Sheffield had, despite the recent difficulties, become an area where only the difficult to manufacture and therefore more expensive, alloy steels were produced. Gradually, the more basic and commonly used grades of steel ceased to be melted as its producers sought lines that were more profitable. Sheffield remained consistently proud of its metal working traditions and the abilities of both its men and management.

The English Steel Corporation had been formed on 1st January 1929, by the merging of the steel interests of Vickers-Armstrong and of Cammell–Laird. The new company quickly closed down parts of its Grimesthorpe, Openshaw and Manchester operations as well as the whole of the Cyclops and Penistone works. Parts of these last two works had been built to meet wartime demands and were less than a dozen years old when they closed. The small town of Penistone, which had seen rapid growth in employment during the war, was particularly badly hit by the closure.

In a similar manner, two of the city's other major steel companies, Thos. Firth and John Brown, merged their steel making interests and would soon enter into a partnership with English Steel Corporation for the production of stainless and heat resisting steels. This joint company, Firth-Vickers Stainless Steels Ltd., became responsible for developing and marketing stainless steels and out of its research into high performance steels would develop those exotic alloys needed for Frank Whittle's first gas turbine aero engine; the development of which would, post 1945, further revolutionise aviation.

Hadfield's remained, avowedly independent and was unwilling to leave the armaments sector entirely. In the 1920s military orders had been very small and whilst it placed more emphasis on commercial work, military research never ended. In the 1930s, as part of this research, they were responsible for the development of an advanced, long range, armour-piercing shell for the Admiralty.

The new company of Firth-Brown soldiered on with its military work continuing to meet the small orders which a cash strapped Admiralty and War Office were able to place. In 1935, out of a total annual sales figure of £2,335,583, armour plate contributed £263,842, armour castings £2,359, armour piercing shells £127,212, gun forgings/air vessels £37,104 and bullet proof plate, just £51!

The years of economic depression slowly eased with a general demand for the area's products increasing. This and the effects of a cautious policy of re-armament, beginning in June 1935, allowed the region to share in the beneficial effects of a national economy which, in some areas, had scarcely suffered during the bleak days of 'the slump'. The major producers, often with great foresight, were again investing in modern plant. The nation would shortly be grateful for this.

Chapter Six

Gearing Up for the Continuation War

As early as 1934, less than a year after Reich Chancellor Hitler came to power in Berlin, the British Chiefs of Staff began to believe that Germany was, once again, a potential danger and a threat to the peace of Europe. As a consequence, Prime Minister Baldwin pledged that the Government would maintain parity with Germany's air force as well as retaining a great navy. The Royal Navy had never spent less than £10 million a year on armaments while the Royal Air Force (R.A.F.) figure was £8 million. The Army had been grossly neglected by comparison. With a budget of around £2 million it had, become, effectively, a 'limited liability' army, fit only for colonial service and quite incapable of serious continental intervention. The *Statement Relating to Defence*, first published in March 1935, heralded the ending of the government's reliance upon collective security, and indicated that it was now about to bind itself to the more ancient security of armed force. In Germany, Hitler pointed to the British White Paper as an excuse to introduce conscription, further increase his military spending and generally raise tension within Europe.

Britain's defence spending plans for 1935 showed a large increase upon those of earlier years. These plans had, out of necessity, been limited by economic circumstances as well as the belief that no foreign leader could ever possibly contemplate a further war. Under these plans, the Navy was allocated £56 million, the R.A.F. £17 million and the Army £40 million. Four years later and just before the outbreak of hostilities, the figures revealed the Navy allocation to be £127 million and that of the R.A.F. to be £133 million with a similar amount allocated for the Army. As a measure of the urgency surrounding the re-armament plans, the services were authorised, in 1938, to insist on priority for their work over those of all normal trade. Britain was now spending over 15% of its G.N.P. on armaments and had surpassed that of Germany which, following the Munich crisis, had reduced military expenditure to 10% of G.N.P.

The Sheffield area's share of these orders was significant, as may have been expected, with all local armaments manufacturers taking on labour and gradually recovering their profitability. Park Gate found additional work for its three high plate mill as the 1936 destroyer-building programme got underway. Hadfield's, by increasing its steel melting capacity, increased its arms output five fold over three years. In 1936, the Admiralty placed orders with Wm. Beardmore, English Steel Corporation and Firth Brown for 168,000 tons of finished armour, for completion within four years, at a time when capacity within the United Kingdom, owing to closures and rationalisation, was only some 40,000 tons per annum. So great was the demand for armour plate that some orders had to be placed with steel suppliers in Czechoslovakia. However, the Sheffield companies still booked 75% of the available orders, with the side armour for H.M.S. *Prince of Wales* being completed by Firth-Brown in 1937. Two years later, Firth-Brown was melting 145,000 tons of liquid steel (compared with 79,000 tons in 1934).

The Admiralty, themselves, financed several of English Steel Corporation's expansion schemes. These included, expansion of the Hawke Street machine shop, the re-equipping of the Cyclops West Works and the installation of additional melting and heat treatment capacity. They were not alone in financing modernisation, the Ministry of Supply paid for the very substantial re-equipping of English Steel Corporation's West Machine Shop, in order to turn out tank armour in a vast building programme which saw Britain, by the outbreak of war, surpassing the Germans quantitatively if not qualitatively in the numbers of tanks being made.

HMS Hood *being fitted out at John Brown's Clydebank shipyard.* (Sheffield Libraries, Archives and Information, with permission)

A view of English Steel Corporation's melting shops during the early stages of reconstruction under plans for re-armament. (Sheffield Libraries, Archives and Information, S 09815, with permission)

One of the areas of greatest expansion, resulting from re-armament, was in the field of aviation and Sheffield was almost overwhelmed by the increase in demand for its stainless, valve, magnet and other high performance steels. Some of the earlier modernisation plans had envisaged just such an increase, as well as for the provision of machinery capable of drop forging the more sophisticated types of multi-throw crankshafts modern aircraft engines demanded. English Steel Corporation, as part of their 1936 modernisation programme, had laid down a 15-ton drop stamp, of German manufacture, to produce crankshafts. For this the nation

Drop forging a crankshaft using a large drop stamp at the English Steel Corporation's works. (Sheffield Libraries, Archives and Information, S 02291, with permission)

would have cause to be very thankful, since this machine and two later copies were responsible for producing nearly all the Rolls Royce Merlin engine crankshafts during the ensuing conflict. English Steel Corporation did not stop there, for, as part of the reconstruction programme, a machine shop was laid down specifically for the range of Bristol radial engine crankshafts.

Other companies who benefited under the government's Air Arm Extension Programme were Firth–Brown and its subsidiary, Firth-Derihon Stampings which offered high quality products including new grades of nitriding steels which had been developed in the city's leading research laboratory, Brown-Firth Research. These 'Hykro' steels were being supplied for manufacturing air-cooled aircraft crankshafts and cylinders. Concern over the likely shortages of aircraft steels encouraged engine manufacturers Rolls Royce to suggest to Samuel Fox that they could become a major supplier of these critical materials. In 1938, in response to this request, the Stocksbridge firm installed a new ten-ton electric arc furnace and, following successful trials, laid down two new heat treatment facilities specifically for aircraft quality steels.

Despite the urgency, the nation's expansion plans for the R.A.F. were lagging behind schedule and in 1938, in an effort to reduce the effects of trade union 'craft restrictions', an agreement, very much like the one negotiated by Lloyd George in 1915, was secured by Prime Minister Chamberlain. This agreement, for which the TUC were invited to Downing Street for the first time since the 1926 General Strike, had its roots in lessons learned during the previous war and was one of a number which required implementation in the event of future hostilities.

In the coming war, there would never be anything like the 'shell scandal' of 1915, for the expansion of munitions production had been planned. The country was now much more prepared but even so, its preparedness would often be insufficient or defective and sometimes both, despite the years of study and planning.

Sheffield had witnessed many changes during the inter-war years. In 1939, the city covered an area of 39,586 acres with a population numbering 518,257 comprising 129,396 families. The granting of universal suffrage saw the city swing, politically, to the left with Labour by now in firm control of the Town Hall, hardly surprising given the size of Sheffield's working population. Of the city's seven M.P.s, three were Conservatives and four Labour; the Liberals, as in the rest of the country, had been swept out of power. Only one, Fred Marshall the M.P. for Brightside, lived in the area.

Much of the city's housing stock, which twenty-five years previously had been described as 'pestiferous', had been improved. Sheffield, assisted by generous government subsidies, embarked on an impressive programme to clear its slums, including the 800, by now notorious, bug infested, 'temporary' wooden huts built to house munitions workers in the First World War. Most of these would go in a symbolic burning – a dramatic means of getting rid of the filth quickly. The 1936 Housing Act gave local authorities a series of subsidies to replace overcrowded property and Sheffield took full advantage of it. Within two years, 24,374 houses had been demolished and some 9,500 of the remaining 13-14,000 houses in the central area had been condemned. By the outbreak of war the city had 26,725 council houses and a further thousand were being constructed. Arbourthorne, Shiregreen, Parson Cross, Shirecliffe and Wisewood were examples of the estates of well-built, spacious, houses with gardens, which the city was building. With them were constructed small community shopping centres and fine, airy schools. The public house on these estates was, however, at a premium.

Sheffield still had its two major railway stations; Victoria, with its long station approach by the Royal Victoria Hotel or more

Spacious, airy council housing on Emerson Crescent, Parson Cross - typical of the new estates of the 1930s. (Sheffield Libraries, Archives and Information, S 00753, with permission)

interestingly, by lift from the Wicker and the more centrally located Midland Station in Pond Street. Both offered their own routes to London and other destinations. Trams now ran every two minutes from Hunter's Bar and the main post office was open for business Monday to Saturday from 8 a.m. until 7 p.m. and on Sunday between 9 and 10.30 a.m.

The city still retained some consulates. The U.S.A., Finland, Peru and Sweden were still represented but the decline from the number of 1914 reflected the impact the recent depression had had on the area's export and arms trades. Ten banking companies still vied for trade in the city centre, which was, architecturally, still largely uninspiring. As a part of a scheme to try to alleviate its local unemployment, however, the council had embarked upon a programme of civic works. One result of this programme, the impressive City and Memorial Hall, opened its doors in 1932. The Graves Art Gallery and Central Library on Surrey Street were opened some two years later.

The City and Memorial Halls. Built as part of the City's efforts to alleviate unemployment. The City Hall still bears impact marks of shrapnel and bullets sustained during Sheffield's blitz. (D.S. Dalton)

The Central Library. Another attempt at positive action to alleviate unemployment.
(D.S. Dalton)

Health care had improved quite dramatically since the previous war and, following legislation, the City had more than doubled its numbers of registered midwives. Infant mortality had dropped from a figure of 99 per 1000 live births in 1921, to one of 49 per 1000 in 1938. The Royal Infirmary and Royal Hospital had both been enlarged. Jessop's Hospital for Women was building a new maternity unit and in 1930, a new General Hospital had been created out of the old Firvale Institution. There were now a total of twelve hospitals, including specialist units for the treatment of infectious diseases, tuberculosis and for orthopaedics.

Sheffield, as with other industrial towns and cities had seen a large, inter-war growth in the numbers of Working Men's Clubs and in 1939, out of one hundred and thirty two registered clubs in the city, forty one of them were aimed primarily at the working man. Other clubs, such as the La Plata Club and Institute on Walkley Lane, The

Limes Club and Institute on Barnsley Road, Darnall Horticultural and Ecclesall Non Political Club on Ecclesall Road, declared having no class or political affinity. There were twelve golf courses as well as twenty-two tennis clubs, many of them using the city's well-kept municipal courts. The Empire, Lyceum, Playhouse, Regent, Hippodrome, Tivoli, Cinema House, Wicker and the Palace were some of the theatres and cinemas in the city centre and these had now been joined by large suburban cinemas such as the Paragon, Capitol and the Manor. Attendances in the sixty cinemas were booming and would continue so to do throughout the war years.

As befitted a largely male dominated, industrial society and despite earlier attempts to minimise the impact of alcohol, the area still had seventeen breweries to service its many outlets, including some one thousand and eighty public houses. There were 246 bakers with Broom's having no less than sixteen shops across Sheffield. Each of the city's 720 butchers, and 1,500 grocers, would soon be taking coupons from their customers. A rationing scheme was already in place, merely requiring instructions for its introduction. The district's 160 fish merchants and 720 fish and chip shops would be amongst the first to feel the effects of the war as it was waged at sea and their

The Cinema House, Fargate. One of the popular city centre cinemas. (Sheffield Libraries, Archives and Information, S 08046, with permission)

customers would soon be offered the 'delights' of rock salmon or even snoek as alternatives to cod, the favourite of the locals.

The slump of the 1920s and 30s did not leave the industrial landscape quite as scarred in 1939 as that which was to be experienced in the 1980s. Despite financial losses and very poor trading results the industrial heartland remained largely intact. The immediate area still had twenty-nine melters of high speed steels; thirty-five iron founders; two 'iron masters'; fifteen spring manufacturers; eleven stainless steel producers; six manufacturers of bright steel bars; seventy four steel converters and refiners; four major manufacturers of steel castings; thirteen forgers; twenty-four collieries; 1,040 cutlers; two manufacturers of railway rolling stock; two builders of railway engines; four major electrical engineers; one manufacturer of optical instruments; four glass manufacturers ; three large brass founders and many road transport contractors , manufacturers of engineers tools and general engineers whose fortunes were inextricably linked to those of the area's major manufacturers.

It was with these manufacturing assets, large and small, existing and potential, that, following the expiry of the Government's ultimatum to Germany on 3rd September 1939, the country declared itself, once again, to be at war with Germany. Everyone awaited the expected aerial onslaught of the German *Luftwaffe*. As early as 1935 the Home Office, through their Air Raid Precautions Department, had asked all local authorities to prepare plans to cope with the likely results of bombing, which was feared would kill and maim thousands of their citizens. Sheffield was a high priority target and by 1936 plans were well underway to identify premises for use as first aid, decontamination and air raid shelters.

By the outbreak of war, hundreds of these premises had been identified throughout the city and booklets were issued identifying them and their proximity to the bus and tram networks. Many were in shops, others in churches, schools, converted passageways, trenches and purpose built surface shelters but none were intended to replace the supposed safety of home. Indeed, it was stressed that the shelters were provided for those who were caught in the streets and not within easy reach of home. There was no typical size. Some were large, as in Exchange Street where the Market Hall had a capacity of 525 whilst others such as a surface shelter in Pond Street could only squeeze in ten. The city had estimated that it would need 6,546 air raid wardens and 12,622 emergency workers. Recruitment had, in general, been good except in the industrial East End. Here, the potential threat of bombing was greatest whilst the response had been the poorest, a fact which gave the authorities grave cause for concern.

Chapter Seven

At War Again

Professor J. B. S. Haldane, writing in 1938 about the likely direction of a future war, declared

> *"There is a half a square mile of Sheffield which is more vital for the production of munitions than any other part of Britain".*[1]

Whilst this was true, the same could be said for other parts of the area, which would be drawn into the largest, state directed, industrial effort this country has ever known, as a result of the introduction of measures for centralised control of both the work force and production.

The immediate official reaction, following the outbreak of war, was to instruct all schools, theatres, cinemas and libraries to close and to encourage families with small children to move to safer areas. In fact, plans had already been laid for the mass evacuation of children from threatened areas, so great was this fear of bombing. Gas masks had already been distributed to adults and children alike and the small rectangular cardboard box in which they were carried, over the shoulder, became something of a symbol of the early war years. The race to build air raid shelters, both large and small continued and Anderson shelters were being erected faster than the manufacturers could supply them.

In the machine shops, rolling mills, forges and melting shops of the industrial area, war work became not only the national but also the individual's priority. The work ethic, which had been so apparent in 1914, was still there a generation later, but this time it came with less jingoism and a more stoic acceptance that Hitler and the Nazis had to be stopped.

Many of Sheffield's manufacturers were based around the city centre, which was still the home of the cutlery 'little mester', as well as in the upper Don and Loxley Valleys, but the majority of Sheffield's big steel and engineering companies had their major plants through the Wicker Arches and in the Lower Don Valley. It was here that the vital 'half square mile' was located. English Steel Corporation; Firth-Brown; Jessop-Saville; Brown Bayley and Hadfield's were the largest

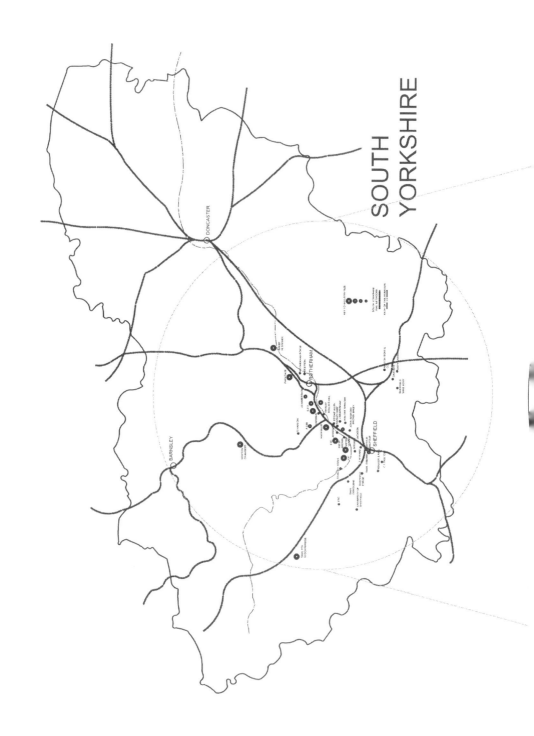

SOUTH YORKSHIRE

KEY TO INDUSTRY SIZE

SOUTH YORKSHIRE
RAIL NETWORK

PATH OF THE RIVER DON

BAKER
BESSEMER

PARKGATE

ROTHERHAM FORGE

BEATSON

ROTHERHAM

KELTON SONS &
CO

CRAVEN UNITED

DAVY

SHEFFIELD
WIRE ROPE

JJ HABERSHON

S.P.T

TINSLEY
ROLLING MILL

S HARLOW

A LEE

DARWINS

EDGAR ALLEN

TINSLEY WIRE

J BEARDSHAW

WALTER SPENCER

HADFIELDS

ESC JESSOPS

FIRTH
BROWN

METRO
VICKERS

JOHN BEDFORD

BROWN BAILEY

SPEAR JACKSON

SHEFFIELD

NEWTON
CHAMBERS

T W WARD

BALFOUR

ARTHUR

SAML OSBORN

STANLEY TOOLS

WALKER & HALL

C T SKELTON

ESC

SAML
OSBOURNE

SHEFFIELD
FORGE

UNIVERSITY OF
SHEFFIELD

BEFORE, DURING AND AFTER THE RAID

FITTING BEDS IN YOUR ANDERSON SHELTER

— and the help that is ready if your home is hit

WITH very little trouble you can make your Anderson steel shelter a comfortable sleeping place for your family. Four adults and four babies, for example, or four adults and two older children can sleep in a standard Anderson shelter, 6 ft. 6 ins. in length.

All the tools you need are hammer, saw, and pliers that will cut wire. The materials are a few feet of timber, not less than 1½″ square, some nails, and some canvas (or hessian, burlap, stout wire netting or similar material).

QUITE AN EASY JOB

Look at the diagram of the arrangement of bunks and you will at once see the idea. The top bunks run from one end of the shelter to the other, the ends resting on the angle-irons that run across the shelter at each end. These bunks should be 20 inches wide, and about 6 ft. 6 ins. long. The lower bunks are the same size, but rest on the floor, on legs 4 ins. high.

THE CHILDREN'S BUNKS

The cross bunks for the children are about 4 ft. 6 ins. long, and have four legs each 14 ins. high, which rest on the side pieces of the upper and lower bunks. The cross bunks can be up to 2 ft. wide. The legs must be nailed on inside the shelter.

Fix canvas, hessian, etc., across the bunks and the job is finished.

These hints are taken from a very helpful leaflet which is being issued by local authorities to all who have Anderson shelters.

SEE THOSE FRIENDS TODAY

. . . and make plans to go and stay with them, or for them to come and stay with you, if either of your houses is knocked out.

Help is ready

If you can't make your own arrangements and you have to leave your home go to a Rest Centre. Ask your warden where one is. There you will get food and clothes and somewhere to sleep. You will be given advice on your problems and help in finding a new home.

If your gas is cut off

There may be a communal feeding centre nearby, where you can get hot meals at very low prices. Find out about it, and if there isn't one, fix up to eat with friends or relations.

Anderson shelter. (D.S. Dalton)

and by far the most important of the steel manufacturers. The contributions and efforts of both their labour and management to the unfolding war effort would be critical for the country's survival.

These companies were not alone for, amongst the small and medium sized companies, who were also established in the valley, were Edgar Allen; Jonas and Colver; Tinsley Wire Industries; Metropolitan-Vickers; Sanderson Bros. and Newbould; George Turton Platt's; Davy United; Darwin's; Walter Spencer; W.T. Flather; Kayser Ellison; J Beardshaw; Tinsley Rolling Mills; Firth Vickers; Firth Derihon; Cocker Bros.; Tempered Spring; Dunford Elliot; John Bedford; Howell's; Spear and Jackson and Arthur Lee. All these companies lay broadly within the valley's confines, which, with a river, a canal, numerous railway lines and depots made a very tempting target for any German bomber.

Further down the valley, in the town of Rotherham, the major manufacturing plants of Steel Peech and Tozer and Park Gate Iron and Steel as well as those of the smaller Rotherham Forge; Isaac & Israel Walker; Robert Jenkins; J.J. Habershon; Rother Boiler; Midland Iron and Steel; Templeborough Rolling Mills; Don Forge; William Oxley and Baker Bessemer added further to its strategic importance.

The valley was defended from aerial attack by a balloon barrage, searchlights and anti-aircraft artillery.

Britain's naval re-armament plans had centred upon maintaining supremacy over the Axis powers but were sadly deficient in producing anything like enough destroyers and escort vessels. These small ships were so important to the convoy system, which, as a lesson learned from the First World War, was quickly reintroduced and an early call to the USA led to the supply of fifty old, four stack destroyers in an attempt to make up this shortfall. The Army was again small by European standards and ill equipped with modern weapons. British tanks particularly were slower and less well armed than their German counterparts and suffered from unreliability. Exceptions were the Matilda I and II (A11 and A12) tanks which, though mechanically reliable and well armoured, were slow and were armed with relatively small calibre guns. The R.A.F. had concentrated on building up its numerical strength, by building aircraft such as the Battle and Blenheim which, in the crucible of war, were found wanting. As the war progressed and the conflict widened, the Sheffield area and the half square mile in particular, became involved in a race to increase output, to aid development of new weapons and to provide radical solutions to both existing and emerging military problems.

No amount of productive machinery or manpower is of any use without a suitable supply of raw materials to work on. As early as the spring of 1940, whilst the country was still in the falsely secure period of the 'phoney war' and just before Dunkirk, those companies involved in supplying special aircraft steels were asked by the Ministry of Supply to form a committee to help sort out any supply bottlenecks. The Aircraft Alloy Steel Emergency Committee was duly formed and consisted of:

Mr. A. Mathews of Firth Brown
Mr. L. Chapman of Wm. Jessop and Son
Mr. Colville of Clyde Alloy Steel[3]
Mr. F. C. Harrison of Hadfield's
Mr. S. G. Newton of Brown Bayley
Mr. G. Steel of Samuel Fox
Mr. H. Williams of Park Gate Iron & Steel
Mr. A. B. Winder of English Steel Corporation
Mr. G. M. Flather of W. T. Flather

Major Senior was appointed to represent the interests of the Ministry of Supply.

A sub-committee, consisting mainly of production managers from these companies, was formed with the addition of two other companies whose representatives were Mr. B. C. Micklethwaite of Firth-Vickers Stainless Steels and Mr. G. Widdowson of Jonas and Colver. Representatives from the Air Ministry and the Ministry of Supply were also included.

It quickly recognized the pressing need to deal rapidly with each shortage as soon as it arose and agreed to pool its manufacturing resources, which though large, were already under stress. One member recorded that, *"the pressure upon us for Government orders is almost … insuperable"*.[3]

They also agreed, in effect, for their plants to be under central control throughout the whole production sequence, with daily meetings to co-ordinate supplies as well as identifying which plant could best produce materials for the latest orders. This agreement was to have far reaching consequences in the future, as the stresses and strains of total war bore down upon the nation and its industry. The supply agreement for aircraft steels was typical of the way the steel companies worked together to help assure final victory.

English Steel Corporation was, by far, the area's biggest producer of engineering goods and, as a part of the Vickers Group, was heavily involved in supplying other group members with steel and

An advertisement for English Steel Corporation. (D.S. Dalton)

components, as well as carrying out group research on such things as improving the characteristics of armour plate.

Other notable members of the group were Vickers Aircraft, which was building Wellingtons, and Walrus aircraft; Supermarine, which was responsible for the Spitfire and the naval yards at Barrow and Newcastle which were building capital ships, aircraft carriers, cruisers, destroyers and submarines as well as gun mountings. Vickers Armstrong had responsibility for major Army contracts covering tanks and guns.

As part of the 1936 modernisation programme, the Company had installed a German manufactured, Beché 15-ton drop stamp, weighing over two hundred tons. This machine enabled English Steel Corporation to produce multi-throw crankshafts, in particular those for the new Rolls Royce V12 Merlin.

This advanced engine was the power source around which many new military aircraft were being designed. The Merlin engine originally developed around 1,000 h.p. and was continuously refined throughout the war. In its final marks it was capable of delivering an output of over 1,700 h.p. Amongst others, the engine powered some of the most famous planes of World War Two including the Hurricane, Spitfire, Lancaster, Mosquito and various marks of Beaufighter, Halifax and Mustang. Employing two teams of eight men per shift, English Steel's Beché drop stamp, when running at full capacity, was capable of stamping eighty-four Merlin crankshafts per shift. For the first eighteen months of the war, Rolls Royce was reliant on this one machine for their Merlin engine crankshafts. This machine, followed by two similar but larger ones built (without German permission) during the war, produced the vast majority of the many thousands of Merlin crankshafts; indeed every Merlin powered Spitfire had a crankshaft made at the River Don Works. The Beché stamp was so important to the war effort that it was guarded at all times but, even so, rumours abounded, after the war, that attempts had been made to sabotage it by placing sand in the hydraulic system. Apocryphal or not, one thing is certain, without this machine, Britain's prospects for eventual victory would have been very bleak indeed.

English Steel Corporation was not only employed in making tens of thousands of crankshafts for Rolls Royce but they were also committed to forging and machining similar numbers for Bristol, Britain's other large aero engine manufacturer, whose range of radial, air-cooled engines powered many British aircraft. Amongst these were the Beaufighter, Swordfish, Stirling, Hampden, Halifax and

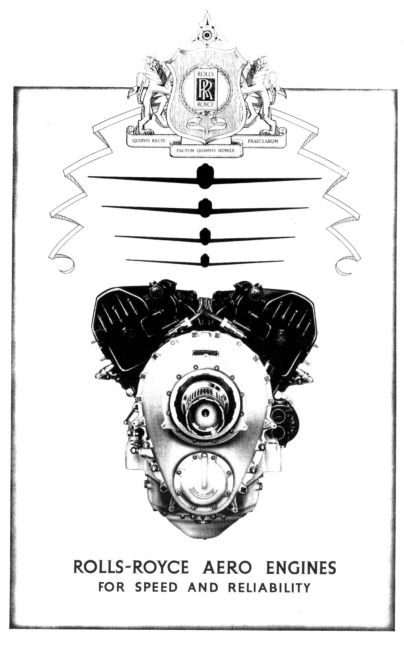

An advertisement for Rolls Royce Aero engines and INSET the Merlin engine on show at Kelham Island Industrial Museum, Sheffield. (D.S. Dalton)

The lower section of a Rolls Royce Merlin engine crankshaft die and a crankshaft 'as forged'. (D.S. Dalton)

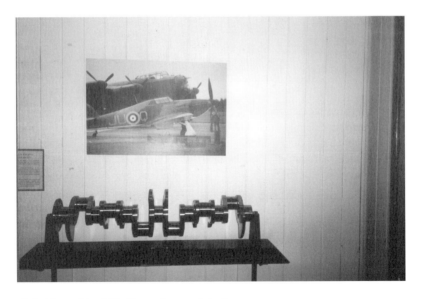

A finish machined Merlin engine crankshaft. (D.S. Dalton)

An advertisement for Bristol aero engines. (D.S. Dalton)

Wellington. English Steel Corporation's contribution to winning the war in the air didn't stop there for, in addition to crank shafts, they produced a whole range of special steels and forgings for the aircraft industry including: gears, undercarriage components and armour plate.

English Steel's forgings were also in great demand by the Army, and amongst others, they were supplied for the 'flail' tank, one of the so called 'funnies' which, when the time came to take the offensive on land, saved many lives by clearing a way through minefields for advancing armour and infantry. They were also responsible for producing forgings for all types of tanks and military vehicles including thousands of lorry rear axles. By the end of 1940, they were fully occupied with an enormous programme of work from the Ministry of Supply.

The Vickers organisation was a major manufacturer of all types of military ordnance, with a vast and diversified commitment for all of the services. In the previous war, the River Don Works had been a major supplier of gun forgings and this role continued. They would eventually supply 40% of all Vickers' wartime gun barrel production. These ranged in size from the small 20mm Hispano aircraft cannon, up to huge 16inch naval guns, designed for use on the four Lion Class battleships. These vast ships had been authorised to be laid down under the 1939 White Paper on Defence but, in the event, were never completed. English Steel Corporation's particular responsibility was for the 17-pounder anti- tank gun barrel, forging 50% of all those produced during the conflict.

Even damaged naval propeller shafts, most notably those of the battleship H.M.S. *Valiant*, which had been damaged by the Italians in Alexandria, were sent to Sheffield for repair under their heavy forging presses, rather than being consigned to the scrap yard.

The Corporation had a long history of producing armour plates and the company had emerged to become one of the world leaders in this field. Throughout the war it was under contract to melt, roll, machine and heat-treat armour plate for naval ships, gun mountings, and to build the hulls and turrets of a number of tanks. These included the Churchill, Cromwell, Valentine, Comet and Centaur.

The company's armour plates were to be found in combat on land and at sea, as well as in the air. Here they were supplied to the R.A.F. where, amongst others, fighter pilots were provided with a measure of protection with seat and head armour.[4]

Dr. Barnes Wallis, whose employment by the Vickers group resulted in his early airship designs for the R9 and R100, went on to develop a

A Comet tank of 3rd Royal Tank Regiment advancing into Germany in 1945. The Comet was one of many tanks to have its turret cast in Sheffield. This example carries the legend 'Calais' which marks 3 RTR's first engagement of World War Two at Hames Boucres south of Calais on 23rd May 1940. (D.S. Dalton)

novel form of airframe construction, the 'geodetic' system, which was used to build the Wellesley, Wellington and Warwick bombers. His fertile mind then turned to providing the RAF with some of the most innovative and destructive airborne weapons ever built.

In the weeks following the evacuation of Allied forces from Dunkirk, when every available weapon in Britain was being sought out to defend a country facing the threat of invasion, Dr. Barnes Wallis was planning for the future. He recognised that conventional bombs could not damage some targets such as coalmines and oilfields permanently. He began to consider new methods by which these could be destroyed. His initial calculations showed that a streamlined bomb, weighing some ten tons, would destroy the target by penetrating the earth to a great depth; the resulting explosion creating a large pressure wave sufficiently strong to destroy the target as surely as a direct hit. This was the genesis of the 'earthquake' bomb.

In early August 1940 English Steel Corporation became involved in the project when Dr. Barnes Wallis, having had the project approved by Lord Beaverbrook, visited Sheffield to discuss technical details. He was particularly concerned about the grade of steel required to withstand the huge stresses of impact, without rupturing the relatively thin-skinned bomb casing. Interest in the project waned, however, and after three years all there was to show was a sample casing for a 4,000 lb bomb which was to have been carried on a Wellington bomber on an experimental 'drop'. In the summer of 1943 the Ministry of Aircraft Production revived interest in the project and a scaled down 12,000-pound 'Tallboy' bomb – the casing of which had been cast by English Steel Corporation – was ready for service in less than a year. Falling with a terminal velocity of 3,600 feet per second, the weapon had the penetrative power of an armour-piercing bomb but more importantly, had the explosive capacity of a large blast bomb. It was first used operationally by specially modified, 'Tallboy' carrying, Lancasters of No.617 squadron, which bombed and destroyed the Saumur railway tunnel. This mission was carried out as a part of the strategy of preventing German reinforcements reaching the fighting in Normandy following the D Day landings.

Demand soon grew for the production of the original 10-ton bomb, christened 'Grand Slam'. With only one experimental drop, the bomb was then used against the Bielefield viaduct. This target had already been subjected to several earlier raids in which over 3,000 tons of bombs had been dropped, to little effect. The viaduct was destroyed by one 'Grand Slam' bomb, fully vindicating Barnes Wallis's theories. In all, forty-one of these bombs, with a charge/weight ratio of 42%, were dropped on enemy targets before the end of the war. An example of this huge weapon's casing – over 25 feet long – may be seen at Sheffield's Kelham Island Industrial Museum.

Barnes-Wallis's third super weapon was his famous, spinning and bouncing dam-buster weapon. The history of its development and its heroic use by 617 Squadron against the Eder, Moehne, Sorpe, Lister and Schwelme dams on the night of 15th May 1943, has been the subject of much writing and is beyond the scope of this book. The weapon's design though, was an object lesson in problem solving and therefore not untypical of much war time development work undertaken by the Sheffield area's engineers, designers and metallurgists, a feat which was all the more remarkable at a time when experienced personnel were at such a premium.

English Steel Corporation was itself a conglomerate, with individual divisions and manufacturing plants making a wide variety of steel products. Amongst these was the Grimesthorpe works, which made a wide range and types of spring. These found their way into all manner of military hardware including, guns, tanks, carriers and lorries as well as the railway industry which, sixty or so years ago, played a vital role in moving wartime supplies around the country. The company's cogging and rolling mills produced hundreds of thousands of tons of billets and bars, which in turn, went into a multitude of military and civilian necessities. Its steel foundries, which have already been mentioned in connection with the production of Barnes-Wallis's super bombs, were also directly responsible for casting thousands of different types of steel tank turrets, bomb casings and gun carriage components.

The Holme Lane Works where, twenty-one years earlier, Arthur Bennett had worked shifts turning shell cases on his lathe, was now a part of the Corporation's Engineers' Tool Division. Now it turned out reamers, cutters, hacksaw blades, drills and files. These items may not have had the glamour of the big guns or tank components but were an absolute necessity if the war effort at home was to be translated into eventual victory. After all manufacturing relies on tools!

Much of the River Don Works, the Holme Lane Works and some of the Cyclops works are still in existence, most notably on Brightside Lane, from where glimpses can be had of the large gun shop, which was reputed to be as deep as it is tall. Apart from the 'Grand Slam' bomb, Kelham Island Industrial Museum also has on display, in

Sheffield and Rotherham's many rolling mills were fully employed throughout both World Wars. Here a mill hand is putting a large flat bar through the finishing stand. (Sheffield Libraries, Archives and Information, S 10751, with permission)

working order, the magnificent, reversing, steam engine that powered the River Don armour plate mill.

Firth–Brown melted over one million tons of high-grade steel during the course of the war. Of this total, over 60,000 tons were rolled into armour plates destined for battleships, aircraft carriers, cruisers and tanks. Peak production rates for the Navy had been reached in 1938, at the height of the pre-war naval re-armament programme. During the war itself, naval demand never again reached this level. On the other hand, the Ministry of Supply's requirements for tank armour would not peak until 1944. In that year the tank manufacturers were supplied with £1,100,247 of armour plate.

Firth-Brown was one of the Royal Navy's major suppliers and, in addition to armour plates, they also supplied the shipbuilders with marine forgings including tail end propeller shafts, boiler drums, marine crankshafts, marine turbine drums and reduction gears.

It was also responsible for 75,000 tank gun-turret ball races, 26,500 springs, 60,000 gear blanks, 386,000 artillery projectiles, 72,000 forgings, including those for aircraft engine crankshafts, for ASDIC submarine detection gear and anti-aircraft gun predictors. It was also a part of the nationwide manufacturing group responsible for manufacturing components and sub-assemblies, resulting in the revolutionary, floating 'Mulberry' harbours which enabled the Allies, after D-Day, to land men and supplies on the Normandy beach heads without the benefit of conventional harbour facilities.

The unlimited supply of engineering tools became a critical factor in the rate of production for almost everything urgent required by the Ministry of Supply as the war progressed. Sheffield was a significant centre for these products and the Firth-Brown subsidiary, Firth-Brown Tools, soon found itself working very long hours, in common with many others, in an effort to meet the demand for its drills, taps and cutting dies. That demand was so high is hardly surprising, given that a heavy bomber such as the Lancaster required the drilling of over half a million holes during its construction!

The campaign waged by German U-Boats against Allied merchant shipping, created an urgent need to find cheaper and more readily available alloying elements for steel making. How to make armour piercing shot without using large quantities of these imported alloys, was just one of an ever growing list of problems metallurgical researchers were required to solve. Research was also needed to find cheaper and more economical manufacturing methods for a whole range of steel products. Brown – Firth was the research and development arm of the Firth-Brown Group and it had nationally

FIRTH-BROWN

has always worked in close co-operation with aircraft designers

on the development of original (and often unorthodox) designs

for which the British Aircraft Industry is so justly famous

FIRTH-BROWN
SPECIAL ALLOY STEELS

THOS. FIRTH & JOHN BROWN LTD. SHEFFIELD

An advertisement extolling the virtues of Firth Brown's co-operation with the aviation industry. (D.S. Dalton)

Firth Brown's modernised electric steel melting plant in 1937. Aircraft and alloy steels were melted here. (Sheffield Libraries, Archives and Information, S 10039, with permission)

important facilities, which were crucial to the research and development work being pursued. One of its many successes included a new, Nitralloy range of nitriding steel, used in many critical applications including the cylinders of torpedo engines. Another exciting and far reaching result of their research programme was the development of techniques to 'centri-spin' sleeve valves for both the Bristol Centaur and Hercules aircraft engines, a technique in which Firth-Brown was the world leader.

Aiming to achieve greater efficiency Firth-Brown stretched its productive capacity to the limit with some success, including the output of 10,000 steel bars a day and 250,000 engineers tools in one week during May 1941.[5]

With the need to disperse such vitally important production away from Sheffield's vulnerable 'half square mile', Firth-Brown opened a tank armour-plate manufacturing plant in Westgreen, Barnsley and a steel-melting unit at Sprotborough, Doncaster. It also supervised tool-making production at dispersal factories in Brymbo, north Wales and Nottingham as well as nearer home in Halifax.

Little now remains of those once proud works, although one gate, bearing the legend, 'Thos. Firth & Sons Ltd., Siemens Dept', can still be seen on Carlisle Street East as a reminder of past glories.

Brown Bayley Steel Works, Sheffield's fourth largest steel manufacturer, was yet another company which made a major contribution to the war effort. Its open-hearth and electric arc furnaces, together with the associated cogging and rolling mills, forges and presses were responsible for the production of: 2-pounder, 6-pounder and 17- pounder anti-tank gun barrels; racer rings for anti-aircraft guns; forged parts for aircraft torpedo air vessel components and aircraft quality tubing. One notable statistic was the production, during the course of the war, of sufficient steel, either as forgings or steel for machining, to produce over one million rifle barrels.[6]

Brown Bayley was the only major local manufacturer to suffer serious air raid damage when, on the night of the 15th December, 1940 during Sheffield's second 'blitz', a 2,000 lb parachute mine exploded in its works, badly damaging a billet-cogging and three rolling mills. The damage to the plant and buildings was so severe that these facilities could not be fully re-commissioned for a further fifteen months.

The works have now gone, being replaced by the Don Valley Arena, Stadium and Bowl; facilities which were built for the 1991 World Student Games, in an attempt to counter the reverse in Sheffield's economic fortunes following the demise of its major industry during the 1980s.

At the time of the Armistice in 1918, Hadfield's was one of the city's biggest employers. Boasting one of Europe's largest steel foundries it was Sheffield's premier producer of special alloy steels. During the years of slump, strikes and disarmament of the 1920s and 30s, it had tenaciously hung on to its armaments business and its independence; refusing to relinquish either one. Financial problems in the late 1920s had made the latter appear increasingly unlikely but it had emerged intact and still independent. Sir Robert Hadfield had been granted the freedom of Sheffield shortly before the outbreak of war for his notable services to his birthplace and by then the company he had founded and nurtured was already fully engaged in rearmament work. The nation had good reason to be pleased that Hadfield's had emerged from the preceding two decades of industrial depression largely intact. Fortunately, they were still sufficiently well equipped to make another major contribution to the war effort and would eventually melt 793,970 ingot tons of steel during the conflict.

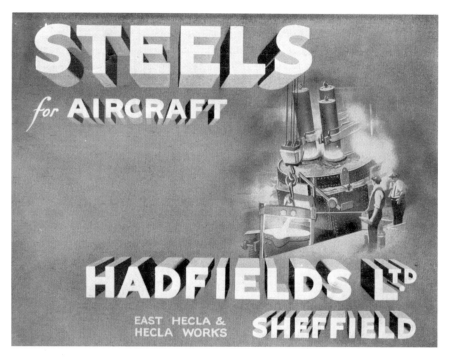

(D.S. Dalton)

As in the earlier, 'Great War', the foundry concentrated on producing shell and bomb cases. During the 1939-45 conflict it was responsible for producing over four and a half million pieces, which utilised 83,000 tons of molten steel.

Hadfield's' ability to produce the full range of shells, in large quantities, was fully utilised by all the services. 1942 saw new types of guns being introduced whilst, at the same time, older models, like the 2 pounder, still remained in service. Hadfield's manufactured a total of 608,857 shells for this gun, before more effective anti-tank weapons replaced it. The average price charged for these shells was 18/- each.

During that same year, the company received the following major shell orders apart from small lots for experimental use.

Size	Quantity
40 mm	300,250
6 pounder	31,956
17 pounder	1,812
25 pounder	81,600
4 inch	48,060
4.5 inch	21,000
4.7inch	5,000
5.25inch	3,000
6 inch	105,606
8 inch	400
9.2inch	5,282
15ins	1,915
Shell caps	550,000

The East Hecla Works was comprehensively equipped with steel melting facilities and out of the 793,970 ingot tons melted there, nearly 50,000 tons was destined to be manufactured into bullet-proof and armour plate. One million of these plates were to be fitted into a total of fifty types of aircraft and gun turrets; including those, which went into the Hurricane, Halifax, Typhoon and Mosquito. Other bulletproof sheets of Hadfield's high manganese steel were supplied for pressing into helmets in massive quantities, as had been the case in the previous conflict.

Another 13,000 tons of molten steel was destined for armour quality castings, most notably for fitting into virtually all the range of British built tanks. The foundry was also engaged in manufacturing aircraft quality castings including those for the under carriage pivot bracket of the Typhoon. Others included a variety of components for the Mulberry harbours and, in particular, the stabilising equipment.

They made the articulated coupling for 'Crocodile' flame throwing tanks as well as casting three million tank track shoes; submarine hydro-plane shafts and steam turbine corrosion and heat resisting blades. Every steam turbine powered battleship, cruiser and destroyer constructed during the war, had its steam turbine blades made by Hadfield's.

The company's forges made gun barrels up to a 3.7inch bore as well as bulletproof rivets. In the early part of the war many British tank hulls and turrets were constructed by riveting armour plates together and Hadfield's was, at the beginning of the war, the country's sole supplier of these specialised fasteners; regularly forging 750,000 a week.

As part of the general plan to disperse manufacturing and increase capacity, Hadfield's was asked to open a separate shadow factory to manufacture 500 lb armour piercing bombs. This was duly established at Swinton, Rotherham but a change in priorities called for far fewer of these bombs to be produced than had been originally intended. Consequently, few of them were actually made there before the plant was redirected to other war work.

Even in peacetime, local companies had co-operated frequently, sometimes to the extent of helping competitors by 'hire working' each other's materials. Hire work was a strong feature of local industrial life, with companies undertaking work for others whose plant may have been unsuitable or too busy to cope. Naturally, with centralised planning, this spirit of co-operation became even stronger during the war. An example of co-operation was the machining of the 'Tallboy' bomb cases so as to utilise all the available capacity. These were cast at English Steel's impressive River Don foundry and taken the short distance to Hadfield's, East Hecla Works where they were finish machined.

There is nothing left now of this large and important site which, at the war's end was employing 10,500 workers, of whom 20% were women. The wartime hustle and bustle has been replaced by a different type of equally frenetic activity, that of shopping in the Meadowhall Shopping Centre.

Jessop–Saville manufactured the usual assortment of typical Sheffield steel products. At the end of the 19th century, its works on Brightside Lane had been one of the city's largest. The company was innovative and, at some stage during the early 1900s had, employed an elephant to move heavy loads, giving rise to the often, unkind local insult, "he (or she) is as big as a Jessop's elephant". In 1939, it was a medium sized special steel manufacturing and engineering company.

Its contribution to the war effort resulted in the manufacture of a host of varied products including, 20,000 aircraft engine crankshafts together with a similar number, which went into the engines of tanks and landing craft. Its G2 valve steel was used in the Merlin aircraft engine and it melted enough to manufacture two and a half million aircraft valves. It also made a major contribution to maintaining supplies of that most vital contribution to everything with revolving parts … the ball bearing. Jessop-Saville alone manufactured over one million bearing rings as well as supplying bearing manufacturers with high carbon, chromium, ball bearing grade steels. Other wartime orders included those for tank armour castings and magnets for radar, aircraft communication and navigation equipment.

It was another local company deeply involved in developing the 'Mulberry' harbours, producing components for the pier heads as well as one hundred tons of gears for pier head winches. These were all ready for installation within six weeks of being requisitioned.

Like the area's other companies, it had a busy war but this did not exclude it from carrying out important research into heat resisting materials, specifically for the embryonic gas turbine engine. What the engine designers wanted was a steel turbine blade, which would operate in temperatures of 7-800°C whilst the blades were revolving at 20,000 rpm. The result of the research, a steel codenamed G18B, was a complex austenitic alloy and it became one of the world's first, successful, gas turbine disc alloys.

The works were demolished many years ago and, at the time of writing, the development of a new riverside complex had just begun.

Darwin's, whose Tinsley works had once been the site of the 1920s Sheffield Simplex car company, was a firm whose pedigree went back to a 17th century involvement in iron smelting operations around Tankersley. During the Second World War, this specialist company initially concentrated on its core activities of manufacturing all types of magnets, including those that aided Britain's survival at sea. Its magnets were used in equipment designed to sweep German magnetic mines from the sea lanes and were also incorporated into British magnetic mines which were similarly laid in enemy waters.

Due to the importance of magnets in modern warfare and with the likelihood of air raids on the factory in Tinsley, a small satellite unit was established at Beighton, then a part of nearby Derbyshire. The holiday coach company, Sheffield United Tours, was contracted to bus in employees from the surrounding area.

Under the pressures of war, Darwin's was encouraged by the Ministry of Supply to diversify and produce other products as well as magnets. This process was successful as, together with its other companies, Andrews Toledo and Wardsend Steel, it manufactured steel strip for gas mask eye piece rims, hundreds of miles of cupro-nickel cladding for armour piercing bullets, smoke shells, anti-tank shells, anti-aircraft shells, cylinder stay bolts for the Merlin engine, steel for barrage balloon cables, bomb grenades, components for explosive mines, undercarriage components, variable pitch propeller hubs and the ubiquitous, 11/14% manganese steel helmet blanks.

The defensive barbed wire entanglements, which had contributed so much to the stalemate and carnage of trench warfare, were once again in great demand. One local company, Tinsley Wire Industries, also sited in the lower Don Valley, were responsible for manufacturing thousands of miles of this wire. It was used in every theatre of war and still presented problems for an attacking force. It also produced anti-torpedo netting as well as twenty three million square yards of steel wool camouflage. Apart from wire and its allied products, it established a manufacturing line to fabricate a total of 750,000 four-gallon petrol drums and 1,650,000 oil drums. It also contributed to the success of 'Mulberry'.

Edgar Allen was formed in 1867, becoming a Limited Liability Company in 1900. It began by designing and manufacturing railway switches, crossings and layouts in the 1880s and by 1900 had established its own foundry. Despite the high financial costs involved in setting up the necessary plant and equipment, the company entered into competition with Hadfield's, its much larger neighbour, in the supply of wear resistant, non-magnetic 11/14% manganese steels. Originally, this steel had been developed for railway and tram points, Edgar Allen producing its first manganese steel layout for the Sheffield Tramways as early as 1903.

During the Second World War, the company cast and machined 1,080 track turnouts in addition to melting sufficient manganese steel to produce 1,115,600 tin helmet blanks. It also melted a range of tool and high speed steels, both of which were in great demand from tool makers trying to keep pace with the prodigious call for all manner of cutting, milling, boring, reaming and drilling tools. To this end its melting shops contributed over 3,000 tons of high-speed steels as well as 3,400 tons of other tool steel grades and sufficient die steel to produce 512,700 cartridge dies, an achievement in itself. High speed and exotic tool steels were, with the technology then in existence, incapable of being melted in anything other than high frequency or crucible furnaces in very small quantities of a few hundredweight.

It also produced sufficient core steel to manufacture 28,114,016 bullets and completed 7,312 tank armour plates to compliment the 872 Matilda and 515 Churchill tank turrets produced. It too had a hand in 'Mulberry', being responsible for bedplates and frames, as well as manufacturing trestle beams for the Bailey bridge.

The majority of the Edgar Allen works are no more. Throughout the recession of the 1980s, as many local companies folded, much of Edgar Allen survived but when, in 1989, the foundry was purchased to allow development of the Meadowhall Shopping Centre, steel melting was moved to Bathgate in Scotland. Parts of the Shepcote Lane Works, where traditional tramway, main line and light rail systems are still designed and manufactured, remain open. The company is now wholly owned by John Mowlem and Co. plc.

On Weedon Street, in the Carbrook area of the lower Don Valley, lay the premises of Firth-Vickers a company jointly owned by Firth-Brown and Vickers, which also owned English Steel Corporation. This joint venture had been set up to exploit the emerging markets for the then recently introduced stainless, heat and corrosion resisting steels. Firth-Vickers was at the cutting edge of stainless steel technology and some of its wartime products reflect this technological lead. The company was responsible for one other site in Sheffield as well as one each in Barnsley and Birmingham.

Together with Firth-Brown, its foundries were responsible for developing the techniques used for 'centri–spinning' in excess of one million valve sleeves for both the Bristol and Napier engine companies. The foundry also completed some 20,000 tons of other steel castings, including 10,000 tons which were of armour quality. These castings were used on Bren gun carriers, Matilda, Crusader, Covenanter, Centaur, Valentine and Comet tanks, howitzer gun carriages, Bofors and other anti-aircraft guns, scout cars and torpedo tubes.

High grade stainless steel sheet was used to manufacture anti-glare, aircraft exhaust manifold cowlings which were fitted to most night flying aircraft and at one point the company supplied this to aircraft manufacturers at a rate of one hundred tons a month. It also pioneered, for tank construction, the manufacture and use of stainless steel welding wire, eventually turning out over seventy tons per month. Stainless steel components for water sterilization plants used during the desert campaigns were also manufactured and its plate mills rolled bulletproof plates.

The development and eventual success of the Rolls Royce engines powering Britain's first combat worthy jet aircraft, the Gloster

Meteor, owed much to the outcome of Firth-Vickers' pioneering research into producing a range of exotic, special steels for critical engine components. These components were required to function in conditions where high temperatures, metal creep and corrosion could quickly destroy less sophisticated materials. The success of the 'Welland' engine owed much to the skill, knowledge and experience of Firth-Vickers' metallurgists and production technologists who successfully overcame the challenges posed by the production of these materials. At the war's end, the British were world leaders in jet engine technology, a position, it could be argued, they still retain.

Vickers had originally acquired the Metropolitan Amalgamated Railway Carriage & Wagon Company with its electrical engineering interests in an attempt to meet the growing business threats of such German companies as AEG, Siemens and the American owned General Electric Company. The new company, known as Metropolitan Vickers Electrical Company, proved to be something of a financial liability for the parent company and in 1928, their controlling interest was sold to the General Electric Company. The name of Metropolitan Vickers was still retained even after the main holding company had become Associated Electrical Industries. Locally, it had one large manufacturing plant situated at Carbrook, in the lower Don Valley, which, like most of the old, industrial South Yorkshire, no longer exists.

The Carbrook works together with a small shadow factory at Bamford, in north Derbyshire were responsible for the design of aircraft electrical generators. These were fitted in virtually all British built aircraft. They built over 140,000 generators as well as components for Fairey Aircraft including the Swordfish, Barracuda and Firefly. They supplied the Army with sub-assemblies for the 3.7inch anti-aircraft gun as well as Valentine tank epicyclic gears. The Metadyne generator, a special type of direct current machine extensively used during the war as a source of power in many servo-mechanisms for gun and radar control, was manufactured solely at Metro-Vickers Sheffield.

Sanderson Bros. and Newbould was one of Sheffield's oldest steel companies. It was typical in that it was not a large concern and not only melted steel in relatively small amounts but rolled, forged and also machined it. Perhaps its most widely publicised activity during the war was the manufacture of the steel for the 'Stalingrad Sword of Honour'. This splendid sword was made by command of King George VI, and was destined to be his personal gift to the 'steel hearted' citizens of that city.

From the largest works in the world devoted exclusively to the manufacture of rustless steels comes much of the steel used in the construction of the famous Westland Lysander and many other leading British aircraft.

(D.S. Dalton)

The Newhall Road works produced over one million armour plates (15,000 tons) including those for the Daimler armoured car. The company also supplied 2-pounder armour piercing shot, paravane plates and cutters, parts for torpedoes, gears for searchlights, clutch plates and components for guns and rifles.

The lower Don Valley had many other small and medium sized companies which all contributed to the war effort. The Tinsley Rolling Mills was a typical case. Employing around two hundred people, it rolled sections for aircraft gun turrets, rocket launcher rails, bayonets and lorry wheel rim and lock rings as well as many thousands of tons of spring steel sections for use in tanks, guns and lorries. It also devoted much effort to the supply of steels for agricultural implements, which, with the German U-Boat blockade limiting supplies of imported food, made agriculture an essential industry for national survival.

Chapter Eight

Beyond the Valley

Sheffield's Wicker Arches mark the beginning or, depending on which direction one is facing, the end of the lower Don Valley. The Wicker takes its name from the ancient meeting ground where wickerwork butts were placed so the locals could practise their archery skills, especially on Christmas Day if local laws were to be observed.

The Manchester, Sheffield and Lincolnshire Railway was responsible for building the arches, which carried that company's main line across the Don Valley from the hills in the west. These were officially opened on 16th December 1848 and at the time, the main arch constituted the largest in the country to be constructed out of masonry. Through the arches, lay much of the rest of Sheffield, with its shops, theatres, hospitals, schools, housing and, of course, industry.

Close to the Wicker lies Millsands. This was the location, where in the 1750s, the Vickers family had originally developed their small iron and steel business. In 1939 the Sheffield Forge and Rolling Mills occupied this location together with their forges, bar and sheet mills. During the course of the war, the company rolled steel bars and sheet for a range of civilian and military uses, which included special products for bomb release gears, barrage balloon cutters, flail tanks, Hispano and Oerlikon cannon shells, armour piercing shot and aircraft catapult components.

As part of the large-scale closure of large swathes of the district's steel industry in the 1980s, the works were demolished and, apart from car parking, the site lay largely empty. It is currently being redeveloped for 'city living', with flats, apartments and other facilities for a new generation of homeowners who no longer have the desire to live in suburbia. A far cry indeed, from Millsands' past industrial heritage!

A notable modern historian, John Stevenson, defined the war effort as:

"*utilising resources to the maximum and allocating them in the most effective way*".[1]

A single ended Rotherham tram makes its way home through the Wicker Arches, sometimes described as Sheffield's 'Brandenberg Gate'. (Sheffield Libraries, Archives and Information, S 07504, with permission)

Viners, a large cutlery manufacturer, was one local firm which turned its hand from non-military to military production, producing such items as smoke bombs, parachute flares, anti-tank gun components, gun forgings – most notably for the 40mm Bofors gun – aircraft components, bayonets and fighting knives.

The Capital Steel Works of Arthur Balfour was just off the Wicker and with other works lying toward Darnall on Greenland Road, and others the company had, for over fifty years, specialised in melting, rolling and forging high speed and tool steels; much of which was consumed within its own engineers' tool manufacturing division. Apart from drills, taps and reamers it also made form tools for cutting propeller shaft splines as well as gang cutters for machining crankshafts. Arthur Balfour was among the pioneers in developing tungsten carbide hard metal, which allowed for much faster cutting speeds to be used than could be achieved with conventional high-speed steels. Together with other local manufacturers, such as Sheffield Twist Drill Company, International Twist Drill and the Stalker Drill Works, they were responsible for 90% of the total U.K. output of twist drills. Between 1939 and 1943, local manufacturers had more than trebled the output of this type of drill. International Twist Drill had even opened factories at Brough, Huddersfield and Bradford with a consequent six-fold increase in its output.

On 15th September 1916, during the Somme offensive, the first tanks had rolled into the history of warfare at Flers. The hulls of those early tanks had been built in Lincoln, from armour plate produced in Sheffield by Spear and Jackson. During the Second World War, amongst a whole range of specialist steel output that company was still producing armour plates for scout cars and aircraft, including those to be fitted as modifications, in the field, to the Mustang (P47), Liberator (B24) and Flying Fortresses (B17) of the United States Army Air Force (U.S.A.A.F).

The humble file was as essential as a sophisticated machine tool was for engineering purposes and an endless supply were needed. John Bedford's rolling mills and engineering shops accounted for the manufacture of fourteen and a half million engineers' and seven million precision files during the war years. Whilst the file was one of John Bedford's most important products, it was not the only product the company turned out. The output of steel from its rolling mills, other than that required for files, amounted to some 34,544 tons including hollow drill steel, which was widely used in mining. It also manufactured 6,050 Churchill tank components, half a million tank

Women file cutters at work at Cammel Laird in 1917. The file, though unglamorous, was a vital tool throughout both World Wars. (Sheffield Libraries, Archives and Information, S 00548, with permission)

bogie axles and shaft blanks, 644,618, 2 lb anti-tank shot and many thousands of gun spikes, blacksmith's tools, spanners and shovels.

Another company with premises on the Wicker was Samuel Osborn, which had moved into the Clyde Steelworks as early as 1868. With the involvement of Robert Mushet in the company, it had been an early pioneer in the manufacturer of tool, die and high-speed steels. By 1939 the firm had melting shops, forges, rolling mills and foundries as well as a large engineers' tool division. Apart from the works in the Wicker, Osborn's had a number of other premises in the region including those at the Regent Works and a shadow factory in Doncaster.

It was the country's largest supplier of the light armour plate used on the Bren gun and Universal carriers. It also rolled sufficient high manganese steel sheet to make over two million, helmet blanks. Osborn's die steels were machined into press tools for use in the manufacture of cartridge and shell cases and their foundry produced bomb cases, armour grade castings for the Valentine and Churchill tanks, tank track links as well as equipment for stone crushing machinery. Amongst the tool division's products were drills and milling cutters, especially those designed for machining Sten, Bren and Bofors gun barrels.

This company, which developed the steel and perfected the manufacture of the Bailey bridge hinge – the critical component upon which this vital piece of bridging equipment ultimately relied – no longer exists. However, its offices are still on the Wicker and are now being used by the Sheffield and District Afro-Caribbean Association, where the sounds of laughter, music and indoor games have replaced the noises of a busy office.

Walter Spencer's was not a particularly large company but it made a laudable contribution to the production campaign. It melted many grades of tool and special steels, including most of that used in the magnetos of the Hurricane and Spitfire, and supplied special tools and drills for manufacturing a plethora of military equipment which included electrically propelled torpedoes, gun predictors and locating pins. These pins were a radical approach to locating aircraft wing and fuselage panels together accurately prior to riveting. They were supplied, in the thousands, to both the R.A.F. and the U.S.A.A.F.

Another of Sheffield's specialist companies was the Sheffield Wire Rope Company. Most of its output was destined for the Admiralty and its Darnall works, founded in 1909, made wire rope moorings for naval mines, mine sweeping paravane ropes and ropes for harbour boom defences. The company had specialised in the manufacture of very long, continuous ropes. Amongst a number of special orders they received during the war were those for a rope, eight and a quarter miles long without a splice and another was for a special lifting sling weighing thirty-one tons, with a length of eleven and a half miles. Coal was then the country's primary source of energy and its extraction was absolutely fundamental for the war effort, the company's contribution was to manufacture colliery winding, haulage and coal cutter wire ropes.

Aurora Gears machined gears for tanks and landing craft as well as parts for 'PLUTO', the pipeline laid under the Channel to connect the United Kingdom with France to supply fuel directly to the Allied forces, after D-Day.

Stanley Tools of Rutland Road was an American owned company that, shortly before the war, had fortuitously supplied their Sheffield works with some modern machine tools. During the conflict these advanced machines were put to good use producing 10,000 shell fuse primers a week as well as a total of 250, 000 tracer shells. With tools of all sorts in great demand, these munitions were produced in addition to their regular production of hand tools. Every British built tank had a Stanley breast drill in its tool kit and every aircraft fitter was issued with a Stanley hand drill! The Rutland Road factory has recently closed.

Two steel forging companies which were typical of Sheffield's many individual, small to medium sized companies were George Turton, Platts and George Senior. Both of these companies had a long tradition and both were involved, in munitions work as well as carrying out valuable, experimental work. This latter work, often in special steels and sometimes in very small batches, was destined for experimental aircraft and aircraft engines. For example a number of stainless steel forgings destined for use on Britain's pioneering jet engines were produced. George Turton, Platts also had a spring division, which made springs for the Riddle Austerity railway engines and the complete range of anti-aircraft guns. Its engineering shops produced aero engine and aircraft parts, airscrew components, tank parts and machined shells. Often going unsung, these companies were frequently short of skilled labour, and worked their machinery to its limits for long hours. Nevertheless, they put their peacetime expertise into manufacturing components for the 'effort', upon which ultimate victory depended.

Another Sheffield spring maker was Ibbotson Bros. whose output found its way into tanks and railway vehicles. This, however, was not all the company did. Their small research department developed a heat treatment technique, which turned a shell of readily available grade of steel into one, which could effectively pierce 4inch armour plate, thereby saving valuable resources.

Darnall lies on a rise to the south of the lower Don Valley and it was where Craven's had established a large railway coach and wagon building works. During the war, it continued repairing and building railway vehicles for both the Admiralty and the Ministry of Supply. These included a series of special wagons, which were used for conveying high explosives around the country. The majority of the Darnall works was, however, given over to military production, including the assembly of Lysander aircraft airframes and wings for the Horsa glider.

Despite having 100,000 square feet of the main assembly area damaged during Sheffield's blitz, its output continued almost unabated. By the end of the war, they had not only assembled various types of airframes and wings but also produced aircraft components for the Welkin, Barracuda, Lancaster and Lincoln as well as manufacturing exhaust manifolds for the Merlin engine. They also completed artillery limbers, gun shields and armoured vehicle gun turrets as well as mobile electric generating plants and ammunition racks and boxes. They also turned, bored and heat treated a range of gun barrels. All this was a far cry from the firm's peacetime occupation of producing railway coaches, which were often luxuriously appointed and fitted out for foreign dignitaries. Parts of the works can still be seen on Staniforth Road.

Keeton Sons and Company converted its Greenland Road works entirely to the manufacture of oleo and piston rods and other aircraft undercarriage components. With the ever-present shortage of skilled male labour, Keetons designed its assembly lines to use an almost entirely female workforce. In 1942, it was despatching 1,200 components a week but this workforce became so experienced that the figure quickly quadrupled. The aircraft parts they manufactured were used in the undercarriage assemblies of the Manchester, Lysander, Beaufighter, Battle and Halifax aircraft.

Davy-United had built up an international reputation for manufacturing and repairing rolling mills, forging machinery and ancillary plant. It continued to do this throughout the war but, in addition, the well equipped machine shops also produced 13,000 tank bogie wheels, 1,500 tank idler wheels, 3,200 tank suspension arms, 2,300 cam shafts and 700 tank landing craft engine crank cases as well as winch barrels for the Mulberry harbours.

Sadly, despite many successful years of trading post war and several changes in ownership, the company is now a shadow of its former self; indeed, its Norwegian owners have sold the head office which, at the time of writing, is being converted into office suites.

Thos. W. Ward had its Head Office in the lower Don Valley It was a very active national company, however, with many branches and subsidiaries, not least of these being Marshall's of Gainsborough.

Scrap steel was acknowledged to be the lifeblood of all electric and open-hearth steel making and fittingly, as one of the country's largest scrap merchants, its role was to collect as much as it could and ensure correct segregation before delivery to the steelworks. In this, the firm was notably successful and can count amongst its many achievements the recovery of ferrous and non-ferrous scrap from one hundred shipwrecks including that of the 56,000-ton *Majestic* and many sunken World War One vintage German U-Boats. The firm was even asked to send a specialist team to the River Plate estuary to investigate the possibilities of recovering the scuttled, German pocket

The Admiral Graf Spee *was one of a small number of German Panzerschiffe, ostensibly built to comply with the weight limit of 10,000 tons laid down in the Treaty of Versailles. In the event they were somewhat heavier. Nicknamed pocket battleships, they were faster than a battleship and more powerful than a cruiser but*

battleship, the *Graf Spee*. They found it an impractical task but were able to recover a number of secrets.

Other divisions manufactured smoke and high explosive shells, laid over one hundred miles of rail track, repaired and reconditioned hundreds of important machine tools, as well as helping in the establishment of shadow factories by moving and re-siting machine tools. They were often able to complete the move and have the machinery working again within twenty-four hours.

this was offset by a lack of substantial armour. The Graf Spee *was laid down on 1st October 1932 and was scuttled following the Battle of the River Plate on 17th December 1939. The relatively thin armour was only discovered after the scuttling.*

Marshall's of Gainsborough, one of Ward's major subsidiaries, manufactured gun mountings and ammunition hoists for a range of ships. These included those for H.M.S. *Sheffield*, whose role in the hunting down and sinking of the *Bismarck* is well known, and H.M.S. *Ajax* and H.M.S. *Achilles* whose gallant participation in the Battle of the River Plate led to the scuttling of the *Graf Spee*. Marshall's gun mountings were incorporated into the main armament of many destroyers, corvettes and frigates. It even built submarines. It is not generally acknowledged but Marshall's was entirely responsible for the building and fitting out all of the 'X' craft, midget submarines, known for the notable wartime exploit of crippling the German battleship *Tirpitz*.

The Head Office, Albion Works, which is just through the Wicker Arches, is now partly used by the Sheffield Chamber of Commerce.

Amongst the many companies based in the centre of the city, C. T. Skelton's contribution illustrates the variety of wartime production. Its shovel shops, naturally enough, continued to turn out spades, shovels and entrenching tools, including non-magnetic types for use by the bomb disposal engineers, whose dangerous occupation sometimes involved dealing with magnetic fuses. Its small hammers supplied shell base forgings for 2-pounder, 6-pounder, 17-pounder and 25-pounder shells, armour piercing shell nose caps and a variety of components for Daimler scout cars, bomb throwers, Napier Sabre aircraft engines, smoke bombs and the Mulberry Harbours.

Walker and Hall, one of the city's most prestigious companies, continued its long tradition of skill and craftsmanship that had made the city's cutlery and decorative plate world famous. It had a showroom in the city centre that displayed its range of high quality, expensive cutlery, cut glass, ecclesiastical and civic plate, trophies and silver ware, in addition to a centrally located manufacturing premises. It had been the first company in the world to produce a useful item by the electro – silvering process. In the year war broke out it was, with a deal of pride, advertising its production of the full range of trophies for the 1939 Grand National meeting.

The war saw them continuing to manufacture a limited amount of cutlery but war work soon became the priority. The majority of the works were turned over to utilising specialist skills. During the course of the war its impressive list of work included, exploder tubes, aircraft air intakes and exhaust ducts, aircraft radiator parts, exhaust ducts – including all those for the Fairy Barracuda; Merlin engine header tanks for, amongst others, the Lancaster bomber and air crew seats for both the Lancaster and Mosquito. Forgings for Bren gun carriers were also manufactured.

The Howard Street premises of Walker and Hall, which sustained damage during the Sheffield blitz, are no more.

Even the University of Sheffield played a part. In the dark days of 1940, with the threat of invasion ever present, the Department of Fuel Technology assembled thousands of Molotov Cocktails for use, in that eventuality, by the Home Guard.

Although both Stocksbridge and the Wortley Rural District are now a part of greater Sheffield, this change only came into force as a result of the 1970s boundary changes, which greatly increased the

A group of female workers pose during a break from their labours at the English Steel Corporation in 1942. (Sheffield Libraries, Archives and Information, S 09245, with permission)

city's area. Until then, they had both been a part of the West Riding of Yorkshire; both communities enjoying their independence from their larger neighbour yet both equally happy to share its facilities.

The Wortley District lies just to the north of Sheffield and the extraction of coal and the smelting of local iron in this area makes it a good example of Britain's early pattern of industrialisation. George Newton and Thomas Chambers had their roots in Sheffield but in 1793, they leased land at Thorncliffe from the Earl Fitzwilliam, to mine local iron and coal and build a foundry. In 1881, the company was registered as Newton-Chambers and Co. Ltd. with both its headquarters and major plants sited at Thorncliffe, Chapeltown. Over the years, the concern expanded, becoming involved in many industrial activities, not least of which were the four coalmines in its ownership lying on the coalfield between Barnsley and Rotherham. During the Second World War these collieries, between them, produced some six million tons of coal. Of this amount their own coal carbonisation and chemical works converted 25% into fuels, fertilizer, motor spirit, naphtha, disinfectants and eight billion cubic feet of town gas (20% of the requirements of a city like Leeds) as well as one and a quarter million tons of coke.

The company had also diversified from its core activities to become a large manufacturer of excavator cranes and other heavy equipment. It had built large fabrication, erection and machine shops and, shortly before the outbreak of hostilities, had laid down a production and assembly line to build the N.C.K. range of track laying excavator cranes. During the early part of the war, plans were unveiled not only for the factory to continue building cranes, which were urgently needed for the expansion programmes covering new airfields and other military installations, but also to expand their tracked vehicle work. A new production line was dedicated to fabricating the hulls of, and assembling all the subcontracted components, of the new Churchill infantry tank. At first, the tank was flawed; as the Prime Minister himself said, they had named it after him because he was so much like it! Nevertheless, it proved a sound weapon, once its problems had been resolved and, Newton-Chambers were responsible for manufacturing over 1,100 of them.

The Churchill tank that stands on a plinth at the site of Newton Chambers' Chapeltown tank factory. *(D.S. Dalton)*

After 1942 and despite being some seventy or so miles from the sea, the company became engaged in wartime shipbuilding. They did this by turning over their welding and fabricating shops from general engineering into constructing a series of midships section for tugboats, coastal tankers and frigates. Perhaps these individual sections were not as large as those the American Liberty ships consortiums fabricated but they were substantial and Newton-Chambers' contribution was the equivalent of one hundred complete vessels. Their maritime activities did not stop there being also involved, at an early stage, in the two important D-Day projects – 'Mulberry' and 'PLUTO'. They manufactured Mulberry's floating breakwaters codenamed 'Bombardons' as well as the floating, flexible roadways called 'Whales'. The 'Conundrums' were massive floating drums, carrying some 70 miles of 2 inch pipe, which were towed across the Channel, laying the pipeline as they proceeded.

Very little of the old Thorncliffe works are left but, on a modern industrial estate just off the A6135, a green painted Churchill tank stands proudly, on a plinth commemorating not only the past importance of the site to the war effort but also as a tribute to the local community's contribution.

The production of steel has long dominated the community of Stocksbridge. Perhaps that domination is a little less so now than it once was, given the rate of contraction that has taken place within the industry, but the works are still major producers. From the small, Derbyshire, lead mining village of Bradwell, Samuel Fox had come over the hills to Stocksbridge to practise his wire drawing trade in the nineteenth century and in 1851, he established his works in the valley. He was a man of vision, as well as being possessed of excellent entrepreneurial skills, and made his fortune manufacturing wire for crinoline skirts, before going on to shape umbrella frames. Seeing other great opportunities, he then moved into producing steel for the booming railway markets. Establishing his first steel rolling mill in 1863, he then went on to make another fortune. From these early beginnings, the company he founded grew to become a major part of the giant United Steel Companies.

In September 1939, despite being a major national steel producer, the company was still manufacturing umbrella frames, one of Samuel Fox's original lines. The war quickly put paid to the production of that most English of devices. Manufacturing of umbrellas was quickly suspended and the factory space devoted to war production.

The large, integrated, plant, occupying the whole of a valley, was equipped with a range of steel making and processing facilities producing high quality alloy, stainless and aircraft steels. A substantial quantity of its output was converted into high-grade wire and springs of all types in their own plant. During the war, the company increased its heat treatment facilities, added to its melting facilities, quadrupled its output of stainless steels and considerably increased its range of springs.

A spring is basically a device for storing energy and the wartime demands made upon Fox's involved producing many such devices! These included springs for tanks, service vehicles, shell fuses and Bren, Bofors and Oerlikon guns. Later on Fox's was asked to take over and run a spring manufacturing plant based in Keighley that had been under performing. This it did.

Its wire drawing plant drew fine, precision wire, which was supplied for many applications including, aero and motor engines as well as clocks. The converted umbrella production line manufactured cartridge clips, of which two hundred million were supplied for the Browning machine-gun alone. Other work involved making bomb fins, fuse bases and radio antennae for both tanks and aircraft.

Samuel Fox's is now part of an Anglo-Dutch company, which goes under the rather anonymous name of *Corus*. They in turn have been seeking partners in the developing world and had been thought likely to merge with a Brazilian steel maker. Having far fewer employees, but with very modern equipment, the successors to old Samuel Fox declare they are making more steel than ever but despite this, partial closure has recently been announced.

The Stocksbridge valley in the 1930's. Part of Samuel Fox's steel works is visible.
(Sheffield Libraries, Archives and Information, S 11830, with permission)

Chapter Nine

Rotherham and District

Sheffield and Rotherham are very close neighbours; indeed, the two communities almost meet cheek by jowl in places. They also share in the old staple trade of metalworking. Rotherham can trace its engagement in metalworking back to 1161 when monks at nearby Kimberworth were recorded to be operating iron smelters. Rotherham had once been a much more significant community than Sheffield, with a fine Parish church, a Chantry Chapel and Grammar School. It was the first of the two towns to be served by a railway and for years, Sheffield was a place near Rotherham.

One of the boundaries between the two communities was the Blackburn Brook, which eventually flows into the river Don. A number of Sheffield steel companies had found its valley a suitable site for expansion and had built new premises there. Whilst being recognised as 'Sheffield' companies, substantial portions of their works were, in fact, in Rotherham. This led to a farcical situation where, in some factories, machinery was placed, not necessarily in the optimum position, but where it was cheapest rated.

Arthur Lee & Son, which was already well established in Sheffield at its Crown Steelworks plant, had built the modern Trubrite Works in this valley. At the outbreak of war large parts of its buildings were painted over in a disruptive camouflage pattern, which remained well into the post-war years as a visible reminder of the conflict.

The company produced steel wire, hot and cold rolled strip and bright bars all of which had military value. Arthur Lee's wire was used in lorry and aircraft tyres, it was supplied for welding rods and for wire ropes as well as being a component of shell fuses. The company produced strip for the portable, channel track (sometimes known as pierced steel planking) that allowed airstrips to be laid quickly in swampy terrain. It also produced coated strip for radio valves and strip to press the cases for Piat bombs. It too had a hand in producing components for both 'PLUTO' and 'Mulberry'.

Records reveal that during the war, the company supplied some interesting orders from the Ministry of Supply. Amongst these were Monel and stainless steel wires, drawn with a streamlined, aerodynamic profile, for use in the aircraft industry and ammunition feed strip. Every British aircraft engaged in the Battle of Britain had its ammunition feed mechanism manufactured from Arthur Lee steel strip and at the height of the Battle, the RAF's fighters were consuming 250 tons of this strip in a nine-hour period. Arthur Lee's Trubrite Works are still there, sandwiched between Ecclesfield Road and the M1 motorway.

Further up the Blackburn Valley, Ambrose Shardlow had established one of the country's largest and most up to date crankshaft manufacturing plants. Its stampings were used in automobile, aircraft and marine engines and, at the outbreak of war, with a work force of around 450, they were making 200,000 crankshafts annually.

The demands of the war dictated a switch from making smaller automotive crankshafts to stamping larger ones for military use. By May 1945 it had manufactured 750,000 engine crankshafts of all types including those for Rolls Royce, Davey-Paxman and Vauxhall Motors. The crankshafts were used in engines to power aircraft, tank landing craft and the Churchill tank.

Steel, Peech and Tozer, or 'Steelos' as the company was known locally, was a founder member of the United Steel Companies. The line of chimneystacks at its Templeborough site was known as the 'Seven Sisters' and quickly became a famous landmark, so much so that 'Lord Haw Haw' remarked upon them during his propaganda broadcasts, threatening on more than one occasion that the *Luftwaffe* would level them.

By 1939 as one of the country's biggest steel producers, with twenty-one, 60-ton open-hearth furnaces, the company was capable of melting 900,000 tons of steel per annum. In this it had benefited from the purpose built works at Templeborough, commissioned during the First World War to help ease an acute shortage of steel. The works melted, rolled and forged general steels, which were used in almost every area where steel was consumed. It also made semi-finished products, which went to other rolling mills or forges around the country for further processing.

During the fighting, the works produced in excess of four million tons of steel. It was the country's biggest supplier of shell steels by far and helped introduce lead bearing free cutting steels for its faster machining. Other shell manufacturers were supplied with 250,000 tons of semi-finished steel, sufficient to produce 609,570,000 shells in a range from 20 mm to 16inch in diameter. This was in addition to what the company was already turning out in the Ickles works. Here was also manufactured many thousands of rounds for 2-

pounder, 6-pounder, 25-pounder, 3.7-inch and 4.5-inch guns. The Ickles works also forged a total of 285,568 gun barrels of all sizes; finish machined the 2-pounder gun barrel and was the largest producer of 6-pounder breech and barrel forgings. It also forged 1,399,986 rifle barrels and, as early as 1942 was producing a greater number of gun forgings than any other British manufacturer. Its forges also produced a total of 484,200 tank parts during the war as well as 124,000 bomb casings and approaching two million ball bearing forgings. Other components were produced for the 'Mulberry' harbours, ammunition boxes and links, Bailey bridges and tank landing craft.

This remarkable set of production figures was achieved by a company which had adjusted to war work from peacetime manufacturing in a most committed fashion..

Parts of the Templeborough and Ickles works are still standing although under new ownership and much reduced in capacity. Perhaps most remarkably, following the demise of steel making, is the adaptation of the Templeborough Works into a 'scientific adventure centre' The Magna Project, which was opened as one of many national Millennium projects, appears to be enjoying some success at the time of writing. As for the Seven Sisters chimney stacks, which Lord Haw Haw had claimed would be laid low by the *Luftwaffe*, these survived until the 1960s only to be demolished as a part of the Steel Peech Electric Arc Reorganisation (SPEAR) project which saw the works converted to the more efficient electric steel making method.

Park Gate Iron and Steel Company occupied a very long established iron and steel making centre and, indeed, the company's antecedents had rolled some of the first plate for the early British naval ironclads. However, changes in trading patterns had meant that, by 1939, it was no longer involved in melting armour grade steels. Early on in the war, with ominous shortfalls in supply looking likely, the Steel Industry Armour Supply Committee was looking for new suppliers. Recognising that the company was already hire rolling armour plate for other Sheffield producers a request was made for it to make trial casts of this grade of steel, hoping that the supply position would be eased by its inclusion in the list of suppliers. Park Gate's trials were a huge success. It began to melt and roll armour quality steel, which was then shipped into Sheffield for machining and heat treatment.

Plate was produced for numerous types of armoured vehicles along with billets for armour piercing shot as well as aircraft

components, cartridge cases and, amongst their less obviously
military products; steel pit props, constructional sections and plates
for shipbuilding.

Donald Bailey, a native of Rotherham, pupil of the town's ancient
Grammar School and latterly a student at Sheffield University was,
in 1936, working for the Army's Experimental Bridging Unit. This
unit was attempting to improve and adapt a First World War
bridging method so that it might be used to carry the much greater
weights of the fighting vehicles then in service. All waterways are,
potentially, natural defensive positions and can cause an attacking
force considerable delay as well as high casualties in attempting to
cross them. The vintage 'Ingus' pontoon bridge was difficult to use
and only capable of carrying eight tons so a replacement was
needed. The need was for a flexible system, which could be
assembled quickly and easily and could carry up to seventy tons. A
replacement system became a priority when, in the retreat to
Dunkirk in 1940, most bridging equipment had to be abandoned in
France.

At an early stage, Park Gate was involved in the experiments being
carried out by the Experimental Bridging Unit. In 1937 the
company was asked if it could roll a 4ins x 2ins inch steel channel
section, ensuring its profile was dimensionally accurate consistently
and to cut them, without fash, to accurate lengths. Bailey's design
for a lattice girder bridge, using modular panels in various
combinations, with only three types of fixings and which, by using
panels in different combinations, allowed a wide range of crossings
to be spanned, was judged a success. By that time Park Gate was
ready to start large scale production of the steel .The prototype was
built in May 1941 by the Braithwaite Company, which was well
known for its modular storage tanks and, eventually, 650 firms
including Littlewoods Football Pools were engaged in the task of
producing 25,000 Bailey Bridge panels every month. Between 1942
and 1945 a total of 700,000 panels were made. Weighing over half a
million tons these panels, if laid end to end, would have stretched
from London to St. Petersburg in Russia!

As the tide of war turned, the Bailey bridge became an essential
tool for the advancing allied armies and they were widely used in the
Far East, North West Europe and in the Italian campaign. During the
latter the army noted, with resignation, that there was always another
river to cross and army engineers built 2,500 Bailey bridges over the
country's many rivers. Neither American nor German engineering
prowess was able to better the design.

Britain had, with the possible exception of the old Soviet Union, the highest wartime direction of labour of any combatant nation. By 1945 over eight million of its citizens were in uniform, a figure almost twice that involved during the First World War, yet despite the widespread direction of men and women into industry, the country was still desperately short of skilled labour. A short introductory course on how to carry out a process could not entirely replace years of experience, yet despite these limitations the contribution Britain's women made to the war effort was an outstanding and necessary one. In 1943, for example, 640 of Park Gate's male employees had left for military service and women were recruited to replace almost all of them.

Whilst Gracie Fields was singing of, "*The girl that makes the spring, that moves the thing, that makes the thingamabob work*", at Park Gate the women who had replaced the men found their work to be somewhat different. Many of the jobs, such as weighing, scrap burning, loading slag, furnace charging, crane driving, welding, steam hammer driving, steel sampling, loco-driving, centre lathe turning, and road repairing, required heavy, manual labour, frequently in difficult environments. Issued with green boiler suits and wearing bright headscarves and turbans the female employees were essential to both the company and the war effort.

The old Park Gate works are no longer there – shops and offices have taken their place – but Corus are still in production, on a site acquired by Park Gate for a new steel plant before the advent of British Steel.

John Baker had acquired the Bessemer Company amidst the economic gloom of 1929 when the Sheffield firm, belatedly trying to modernise their plant, had run into financial difficulties. All activities were thereafter concentrated at an expanded Kilnhurst site, which, after the prudent re-armament plans of 1937, witnessed the location of all shell forging into a new building.

The war years saw the Baker-Bessemer Company engaged in manufacturing a range of shells including gas shells. They also produced anti-aircraft gun mountings, aircraft carrier catapult pulleys and armour piercing nose caps and rocket projectile nose heads. The experience they had gained over many years was put to good use when they were called in by the Ministry to try and solve a problem, which was plaguing the Churchill infantry tank.

This vehicle had been built 'off the drawing board' by Vauxhall Motors of Luton. It was found to be unreliable and flawed as a consequence. One such fault, which Baker-Bessemer solved, was that of the inordinate wear experienced in the tanks' bogie wheels. As designed, its many bogie wheels, which carried tough, wear resistant, high manganese steel track, had been made from cast mild steel but the combination of the abrasive properties of desert sand and the much harder track the wheels were designed to carry resulted in severe wear. Chilled iron castings had been tried but were found to be little better than the originals. A solution to this problem had to be found quickly and Baker-Bessemer was consulted.

Any junior metallurgist might have forecast the inevitable results of this mixture of wear resisting and soft steels operating together in an abrasive environment The company contributed to the eventual success of the tank by experimenting with alternative types of steel to make bogie wheels which did not need replacing every hundred miles or so. Baker – Bessemer's successful experiments resulted in the use of hard chromium alloyed steel for all future production machines. This satisfactory solution, to a problem which ought to have been foreseen, saw the company forging as many as 8,000 of these chrome alloy bogie wheels a week.

Glass might not seem to have much in the way of military value but Beatson-Clarke, with their Rotherham and Barnsley works, made bottles. When filled, their bottles contained drinks, anaesthetics, serums, vaccines, medicines and drugs. Every civilian, serviceman and woman came across a Beatson-Clarke bottle sooner or later during the war. Four million were issued to servicemen, the contents of which made tainted water drinkable within one and a half hours and an additional two million contained anti-malaria tablets.

The company, which had started to produce, hitherto imported, laboratory tubing during the First World War, continued to service not only the military but also the domestic market. Despite its full order books it was able to find time and factory space to produce components for the military, not least of which was the glass sphere for the "sticky" anti-tank bomb. Its engineering shops, already overburdened with plant maintenance and design work, also contributed to the company's war effort by: machining aircraft propeller blades, manufacturing detonator tubes and making dies for casting/forging early jet engine components as well as making tank and aircraft components. Both plants are still in production, making amongst other things, glass bottles.

Robert Jenkins turned its peacetime plate fabrication, boiler making and engineering prowess into manufacturing many items with a more obvious military value. Amongst a considerable list for use by all the services were depth charge drums, submarine rudders and hydroplanes, Bailey bridge sections, flame thrower vessels, explosives side containers for the X craft miniature submarines and anti-aircraft rocket projectile launchers (the Z.Z. batteries).

Soon after the war, when discussing the company's contribution to the effort, it stated simply that, "*we welded parts for making war.*"[1]

The Holmes district of Rotherham is an area steeped in the tradition of metalworking. The Earl of Effingham had erected a works there during the eighteenth century and the illustrious Walker's of Masboro which proceeded to expand and develop the site had in turn, purchased his slitting mill in 1775. Most of the British Army's cannon, used to good effect during the Peninsular War, had been cast at the Holmes works and, in 1815 the company had built the first iron bridge over the Thames at Southwark. In 1829 the company had been sold to J.J. Habershon whom, together with his successors, continued to develop it to such an extent that in 1939 it was the largest producer of accurate, cold rolled strip in the United Kingdom and was one of the few companies capable of producing mild, carbon, alloy and stainless steels down to a thickness of .0015-inch.

The steel strip produced was used to manufacture a range of products from razor blades to cameras and telephone and radar equipment. Most significant of all, perhaps, was its specialisation in the production of aircraft steels. The company first became involved in this developing market when they supplied the stainless steel for the spars of the ill-fated R101 airship. In the early 1930s, their publicity proudly proclaimed that they were, "*the firm that made the (British) all metal aircraft possible*".[2]

In this, they were referring to the Bristol Bulldog fighter, which was introduced into service with the R.A.F. in May 1929 and referred to its all-metal airframe.

It was a very substantial contributor to wartime aviation with its aircraft grade steels being found in every British built aircraft, including the stainless steel engine bays of the pioneering, jet powered, Gloster Meteor fighter. After more than two centuries of metalworking, the works closed in 1981.

Apart from steel, glass and coal mining, Rotherham also had a long and proud history of producing brass products. Gummers, Guest and Chrimes, W. N. Baines and A. T. Green produced all manner of brass components and fittings, especially those for use in marine environments. Consequently, these brass ships fittings, water gauges, valves; glands and lubricators were all in great demand from wartime naval constructors and ship repairers. The firms also manufactured brass fittings for wartime civil engineering and railway projects, including those fitted to the Riddles and Bulleid 'Austerity' locomotives.

Chapter Ten

The Sheffield Gun Defended Area

Sheffield and Rotherham were both expected to become early, major targets for the *Luftwaffe*, especially due to the concentration of so many of the vital, major armaments works within the confines of the Don Valley. After the Fall of France in June 1940, the threat was even greater, given that the Germans had captured air bases in France, the Low Countries, Denmark and Norway.

The Sheffield Gun Defended Area was designed to give the city and its region an element of defence against aerial attack. It was

Barrage balloons being flown from the R.A.F's barrage balloon site at Crookesmoor in early 1940. (Sheffield Libraries, Archives and Information, S 03559, with permission)

responsible for anti-aircraft defences, and consisted of anti-aircraft artillery, searchlights and a balloon barrage. As originally established it was both insufficient and inadequate to protect the area but was nonetheless, all that could be provided in the early years of the war.

Initially, the 57th Anti-Aircraft Brigade, Royal Artillery (York and Lancaster Regiment) manned the area's three gun sites and in April 1942, they began to be supplemented by locally recruited units of the 12th Anti-Aircraft Home Guard Regiment, equipped with twin rocket projectors (Z Z batteries). These rocket batteries were initially sited at Shirecliffe, Brinsworth and the Manor and in January 1943 they were reinforced by 171st Heavy Anti-Aircraft Battery, posted to sites at Malin Bridge, Norton, Wentworth and Thrybergh. In all a total of 185 twin launchers were based in the area and these were manned, nightly, on a rota basis, by a total of some 5,400 men who were also expected to carry out their normal occupations! This therefore, precluded any members of the Home Guard who were already working shifts.

The first headquarters of the Sheffield Balloon Barrage was established at 641, Attercliffe Road, Sheffield, but soon moved to a

A ZZ anti-aircraft rocket battery. Shirecliffe, 1944. (Sheffield Libraries, Archives and Information, S 02559 and Sheffield Newspapers, with permission)

An anti-aircraft gun emplacement on Warminster Road in early 1940. Note the location equipment in the foreground and the 3.7-inch gun in the background. (Sheffield Libraries, Archives and Information, S 03553, with permission)

disused confectionary factory on Bridge Street. Finally, it moved to Number 16 Balloon Centre at R.A.F. Norton, where facilities were incomplete on the outbreak of war. Locally recruited units of the Auxiliary Air Force deployed to their wartime positions from their first headquarters, upon the orders to mobilise. Number 939 Squadron, responsible for the western area, went to Broom Grove Road; Number 940 Squadron went to Rotherham, establishing its Headquarters in the town's Station Hotel, whilst Number 941 Squadron positioned itself in the middle of the zone on Scott Road.

The remains of the anti-aircraft gun emplacement on Shirecliffe Hill in the late 1990's. (D.S. Dalton)

The view of the city centre from the Shirecliffe anti-aircraft gun site in the late 1990's. (D.S. Dalton)

In addition, an attachment of W.A.A.Fs from Number 34, (County of York) Squadron was posted to Headquarters.

The Barrage was flown operationally, for the first time, on 26th August 1939 and at full strength, could fly a total of 72 balloons, each of them measuring some 63 ft by 31ft, at a height of around 6,000 ft. The balloons were all operated from motorised winches, crewed by ten men. With the ever-growing shortage of manpower, an argument was made for these operations to be carried out entirely by WAAF.s. After much debate, it was decided to experiment with an all female crew to see if they could cope with the potentially hazardous and heavy work involved. The Sheffield area's Barrage was chosen as the site for this experiment, which proved a notable success, and by the end of 1941, thousands of W.A.A.F's together with their NCOs and officers were taking over balloon barrage sites throughout the country.

The first German bomb fell on Sheffield on 18th August 1940 and a day later, the B.O.C. plant in Rotherham received a direct hit. These small, initial raids were the first of a total of sixteen attacks across the area from Dore in the west to Rossington in the east during which 785 people were killed or reported missing and a further 1,817 injured.

A view of Carlisle Street after the Sheffield blitz. (Sheffield Libraries, Archives and Information, S 01256, with permission)

Sheffield's 'Moor' suffered heavy damage during the blitz. John Atkinson's department store was completely destroyed. (Sheffield Libraries, Archives and Information, S 01238, with permission)

Damage to South Yorkshire's already poor housing stock was severe with 77,624 homes being destroyed or damaged. The majority of the area's casualties occurred in Sheffield on the nights of 12th/13th and 15th December. These two raids – the 'Sheffield Blitz' – saw the city suffering the same fate that had befallen London, Coventry, Southampton, Birmingham and many other cities and towns.

The German aviators were helped to find their targets by blind bombing devices, the *Knickebein* and the more sophisticated *X-Gerät*, which, by using radio beams, indicated the exact point of bomb release and could be operated automatically. With a full moon,

The Wellington Inn, Brightside Lane (now demolished) was where the German navigation beams were alleged to intersect. (Sheffield Libraries, Archives and Information, S 07008, with permission)

a clear sky and a keen frost, the night of the 12th/13th December 1940 provided almost perfect conditions for the raiders. The target must have been very clear. However, after a raid of nine hours duration by 280 aircraft, during which 450 high explosive bombs, six parachute mines and thousands of incendiaries were dropped, almost all landed on civilian targets. This was a far cry from the German communiqué which claimed that the targets had been steel and war factories. The blind bombing, radio beams were capable of

Public Notices.

COUNTY BOROUGH OF ROTHERHAM.

Public Air Raid Warning Sirens

NOTICE IS HEREBY GIVEN that the Public Sirens In Rotherham will be tested at 10 o'clock in the morning, on Monday, 3rd July, 1944.

The Sirens will sound a steady note for one minute, followed by two minutes silence; the warbling note for one minute followed by two minutes silence, and then a steady note for one minute.

This is for the purpose of testing the working of the Sirens, and no action should be taken by members of the public.

CHARLES des FORGES,
Town Clerk and Air Raid Precautions Controller

(D.S. Dalton)

being bent by electronic counter measures and it has been suggested by Ronald Fairfax that the civilian areas of Sheffield were sacrificed to save its vital factories.[1]

Another raid on the 15th December was of much shorter duration, starting at 6.50 p.m. with the 'all clear' being sounded at 10.17 p.m. and this time it concentrated on the industrial East End of the city. The bombs were dropped in six waves, by a total of seventy-seven aircraft flying in a line from Arbourthorne to Grange Lane on the Rotherham boundary. About 100 high explosive bombs were mixed in with thousands of incendiaries and five parachute mines. One of these mines was to cause the only long lasting damage to armaments production in the area, when the Brown-Bayley rolling mills were severely damaged. The other aerial mines caused damage to a number of works, including parts of English Steel Corporation,

Hadfield's and Steel, Peech and Tozer as well as a railway station. Firth-Brown suffered some bomb damage and was forced to cease steel making for a short period in order to repair the melting shop roof. Other firms, whilst not directly damaged, had to wait until a number of unexploded bombs could be made safe. One that landed at George Turton, Platt's could not be removed until the end of December.

The effects on the area's war production were relatively light, given the ferocity of the raids. Though there was extensive bomb damage, many firms suffered only short term losses in production but the city's infrastructure had been severely dislocated. Electricity supply dropped from 167,750 KW on 12th December to 65,000 KW on the 16th. Lowering of demand due to damaged premises caused much of this but with an enormous effort supplies were almost all reconnected within fourteen days. At the end of the month, supply was back up to near normal at 145,500 KW. The gas supply situation was also a serious problem with damage to the network again causing severe disruption. Eight gasholders were put out of action and 550 trunk and distribution gas mains from 3-48 inches in diameter were damaged. The city's extensive sewerage system had also been quite badly damaged: ninety sewers requiring extensive repairs. Another potentially serious problem caused by the bombing, not least to the health of the community, was the damage to the water distribution network. This had, in parts, failed completely during the raids and over 300,000 properties were left without water until repairs could be made.

On the mornings after the raids people from all over the city attempted to make their way to work. With the public transport system in chaos, and with the constant danger of unexploded bombs, Sheffield's residents often walked miles through badly damaged streets, to find, perhaps, a pile of rubble at the end of the journey. On their journey they would meet others who had worked nights, anxiously making their way home wondering what they might find when they eventually got there. Doctors' surgeries were very busy. Stress, strain and fear were frequently manifested in psychosomatic conditions such as rapid hair loss, which others feared might be contagious.

No evidence exists to show that the defending guns seriously damaged a single German aircraft although the fall out from their shrapnel did much damage to both property and the balloons! One side effect of the blitz was the addition of looting to the city's 1940 Crimes against Property statistics. To the five cases of burglary, 87 of housebreaking, 192 of shop breaking, 22 of attempting to enter, 33 of entering with intent, must be added the 371 cases of looting. Of these incidents the hard-pressed police were able to solve 144 cases, and found that juveniles had committed 95 of them!

The Sheffield area endured its last air raid on 28th July 1942, but its anti-aircraft defences would remain on alert for the years to come and the Home Guard wasn't finally stood down until December 1944.

Chapter Eleven

A People's War

The war in Europe ended following the unconditional surrender of German forces on 7th May 1945. Winston Churchill announced the news to the House of Commons the following afternoon. The war against Japan would continue until the 14th August, when, following the use by the Americans of two nuclear bombs, the Japanese capitulated. News of the ending of the war was greeted with enormous relief, joy and sadness for all those who had suffered or died. At Firth-Brown, a shift of tool workers had a spontaneous party and images of Hitler were hung from the factory ceiling to the acclaim of all and sundry. Peace, at last, with all its prospects, hopes and doubts fell across a joyous country.

The Battle for Production involved all of the area's manufacturers and indeed some, which, prior to the war, would never have considered themselves vital to anything other than their shareholders. Whether their contributions were great or small they all played a part in the 'effort'. Some were able to concentrate on manufacturing one or two items whilst others had made a variety of components.

In the final year of the war, national expenditure had amounted to £6,179.5 million of which 82.945% of this figure had been used to finance the war itself. In total, the conflict had cost the country £28,000 million. This amount was two and a half times the total financial cost of the First World War. The Second World War had seen a ten fold increase in Britain's output of small arms and shells; gun production had grown seven and a half times; the production of wheeled vehicles by three and a half times and the number of bombers had grown ten fold. Six million tons of merchant vessels and half a million tons of major naval vessels had been built.

Despite the prodigious industrial effort and the sometimes-coercive measures to direct labour, including the mobilisation of young women to either join the armed forces or take up war work, it is worth noting that the war could never have been won without the massive assistance of the United States. British industry and its infrastructure were outdated equally and were worked to the point of exhaustion. It was never able to match the productivity per employee of the Americans or, indeed, of the heavily bombed Germans. Such

Sheffield children celebrating VE day in 1945. (Sheffield Libraries, Archives and Information, S 02389, with permission)

A VE day street party. Somehow rations were stretched to provide the 'treats'.
(Sheffield Libraries, Archives and Information, S 03622, with permission)

was the strength of the American economy and its ability to produce weapons on a vast scale that by the end of 1943 their munitions output alone, was four times that of the U.K. They were supplying 50% of our tanks; 75% of the tank transporters; 66% of the transport aircraft and almost all of our tank landing craft, to say nothing of food supplies.

Realistically, in 1939, despite earlier, optimistic re-armament plans the British were militarily unprepared for total war and were even less so financially. The nation simply could not afford to fight a long war on its own and was utterly dependent upon the French holding the Germans until the re-armament plans bore fruit. As it turned out, the French could not halt the Germans and by March 1941, Britain's financial resources had gone. The country was bankrupt, to be rescued at the last moment by the US offer of Lend-Lease. In the last year of the war, Britain was overspending its income, which had largely been derived from taxation and forced borrowing from the population by £2,100 million a year. The shortfall had been derived from three sources; Canadian Mutual Aid, Sterling Area credits and for rather more than half by Lend–Lease.

The population, in general, had been mobilised to an extent hitherto unknown, with many taking on roles for which their lives up to that point had provided little, if any, experience. Government policy and propaganda had encouraged the general populace to look upon the conflict as a 'people's war'. There was the anticipation that a post-war Britain would not revert to the pre-war *status-quo*. For many members of the working class the alliance with the Soviet Union was an example of real socialism at work and badges proclaiming 'U.S.S.R. – U Should Support Russia' were commonplace. For some, the hope of a better future would only be realised by destroying completely the old regime of position and privilege.

The lives of ordinary working folk had always been something of a struggle, but the war added to these burdens. Rationing of basic foodstuffs was introduced in January 1940 and whilst a much fairer method than rationing by price it nevertheless took a deal of inspiration and initiative by a housewife to feed a family. In 1945, the weekly basic ration per person had declined to 4oz of bacon, 2oz tea, 8oz sugar, 8oz fats, 3oz cheese, 2 pints milk and meat to a value of 1s/2d (6p). Clothing was also rationed on a points system, and families frequently pooled their coupons for an event such as a wedding. A typical man's suit, made from 'utility' cloth, would require half an individual's annual allotment of clothing coupons. Much ingenuity was needed to try and keep 'smart'. Old clothing was never thrown away but if possible, reworked and young women habitually painted their legs with gravy browning using an eye pencil to give the impression of seamed nylon stockings – virtually unobtainable unless the young lady knew a GI! The policy of the government, as stated by Sir Stafford Cripps, was that "*personal extravagance must be eliminated altogether*" and in working class areas there was little alternative.[1] Exhorted to avoid waste, to avoid travel and to economise on everything from the depth of hot water in the bath to putting clothes away tidily, extravagance, where it existed, was the domain of a very small sector of society.

Long hours of work, often involving shifts and with a reduced number of public holidays were bad enough, but if the extra duties of fire watching or of duty in the A.R.P, Home Guard and Auxiliary Fire

Service were added to the equation, the average worker was left with little time for leisure. Yet somehow the fabric of society never collapsed under the strains imposed upon it and indeed, some would argue that society had never been better. Morale may have been low at times and war weariness was a reality but despite some strikes, most notably by the Kent miners, high production was generally maintained throughout the entire period.

Public houses, clubs, theatres, dance halls and cinemas, apart from the first few weeks, had remained open. Sometimes, the pubs would only serve their regular customers when supplies were low but the cinemas always attracted huge audiences. Dances in church halls, community centres and dedicated dance halls were very popular. Escaping from the realities of a usually dreary and grey daily life was a necessary part of survival. Some public houses situated in the most unlikely of areas put on concerts of classical music. The Wharncliffe Hotel at Firth Park, Sheffield was one such venue. Here artists who, in the normal manner of things, would have given the place a wide berth gave a series of well-received performances. After a few early scares, the working man's game of football continued. Despite many players being called up or volunteering for the armed forces, scratch and guest teams played in re-organised regional Football Leagues but a few clubs preferred to close down for the duration. None of the South Yorkshire teams did so; all of them continued playing in the East Midland league.

Full time work resulted in higher wages for everyone and women's wages, in particular, soared. This, coupled with younger family members' contributions meant that a family's disposable income could have been high. With chronic shortages of almost everything, this was the perfect climate for hyperinflation, a danger of which the Government were only too well aware. Rationing, the imposition of higher rates of taxes and duties as well as increases in all post office charges kept the inflationary tendencies of the economy under control. The perceived excess earnings were later made subject to the obligation of forced lending to the Government. Through inflation these 'post war credits', when repaid years later, were worth only a fraction of their original value. Indeed, it was very much a 'People's War'. They had fought it and they had paid for it!

Plans and demands for a 'New Jerusalem' had grown over five years, with universal health care, education, better housing and full employment being at the centre of a new, planned and optimistic Britain. This new Britannia would be a land that would forever end unrestricted private enterprise with all its cyclical problems and its abuses of labour. A nation, which for two years had stood alone against fascism, now believed it could carry out its own ambitious plans. There was, however, one very major flaw that had not been foreseen, for British reconstruction plans relied, heavily, on the continuation of American Lend-Lease and dependence upon the Americans.

The break up of Britain's wartime coalition government and the subsequent, overwhelming defeat of the Conservatives at the hands of Clement Attlee's Labour Party in the election of July 1945 brought, for most, the promise of better times. The truth though, was that Britain and its industry was in a very poor state, with massive sterling debts and a jaded industrial infrastructure. Reconstruction required the full support and co-operation of Britain's American allies. Through two world wars their economy had grown enormously whilst, contrarily, Britain's had declined and the country was on the verge of national bankruptcy. Realistically, the nation could neither reconstruct nor create a New Jerusalem without their co-operation.

America's unexpected and sudden cancellation of Lend-Lease by their new President, Truman, only days after the end of the war, saw the plans of the fledgling British government thrown into chaos. In August 1945, Lord Keynes stated that the gap left by the cancelling of Lend-Lease meant that, "*a greater degree of austerity would be necessary than we have experienced at any time during the war*".[2]

The resulting years of further effort, of austerity measures, of rationing, of shortages of fuel and of food were scant reward after the years of sacrifice for most of the country's war workers and servicemen. Such was their lot, however, in the immediate post-war period. Yet despite daunting obstacles, not least of which was the state of the nation's finances, post-war Britain achieved many of its objectives; education, housing and healthcare improved, as did pensions and social security benefits. At last, certain sections of the community were seeing some return on their effort expended during the war.

Britain was still left with pretensions of being a global power and keystone of the sterling area: roles it could no longer afford. Instead of trying to carry out rapid modernisation of its domestic and industrial infrastructure it still devoted too much of its wealth in keeping its armed forces on station around the world and anxiously trying to retain the value of sterling. Encouraged by the Marshall Aid offered by its US allies and aware of the Soviet threat, Britain retained many of its overseas forces when, in reality, the financial burden was one that could not be borne. The start of the Korean War in 1950 encouraged a further, costly re-armament programme.

Full employment lasted for almost three decades after the end of the Second World War. Despite the parlous state of its industry, Britain had two decades of very successful, if uneven, competition with its western European and Japanese competitors, then still rebuilding their devastated industrial bases. This easy success encouraged a singular lack of enterprise and judgement on the part of successive British governments and industry as a whole. The war and the succeeding years of peace had distorted the economy's development. Too much reliance was placed upon the old staples of coal, steel, shipbuilding, textiles and heavy engineering. Anything, at any cost, or any quality, was too frequently the cry as the nation attempted to export more whilst endeavouring to balance its trade. Goods were often exported when they would have been best used at home. Domestic steel rationing as a result of exports, bedevilled many post-war modernisation plans and old, overworked plant was run continuously, until it became hopelessly outdated or utterly uneconomic. By then, much of the area's industry could not or would not be rescued. When real competition began, again much of Britain's industry found itself hopelessly overpriced and outclassed. European free trade policies would hammer home these deficiencies.

Many of the country's industrial problems, which had been quite evident pre-war, were left to be faced decades later and with a social cost that could never have been foreseen in 1945. For many older people the cry of, "we won the war but lost the peace", was only too true as they saw the economies and living standards of our erstwhile enemies grow whilst Britain staggered from one economic crisis to another. Large parts of South Yorkshire became an industrial wasteland during the late 1980s as national policy apparently changed to one of ignoring the costs of imports and virtually forgetting our balance of payments. Economic indicators changed to show just how much money we were spending (and borrowing) in the High Street. The human skills and aptitudes that had made the Sheffield area such an important factor in the prosecution of two world wars were largely forgotten and made 'redundant'. Industry, it seemed, was no longer fashionable!

Since the Second World War, volumes have been written, giving very effective analyses of the defects of British war production and, certainly, statistics would appear to demonstrate not only a deal of poor management but, equally, an unwillingness by the worker to produce as effectively as did those of some other belligerent nations. The analyses, however, neglect to mention the parlous state of much of Britain's industry at the outbreak of war. The cost of years of

Despite hopes for a 'New Jerusalem' after two World Wars, many children still experienced poor housing conditions until the early 1970s. (D.S. Dalton)

industrial and social neglect; of under investment and the lack of educational opportunities for most members of the working class, effectively limited their achievements. Posterity will record, however, that for more than two years before the industrial might of the United States became involved in the struggle, Britain stood alone against fascism. The nation's industry and manpower, buttressed by an implacable war leader, showed the resolve, at whatever cost, to ensure that the country did not suffer the same fate as that which befell much of western Europe. The working men and women of this country not only tried to keep family life running but also did long hours in the Home Guard, or on Civil Defence duties, in addition to their regular jobs in the factories and coalmines. That they successfully coped with their lot whilst facing bombing, fear and the likelihood of sudden bereavement is a never-ending source of wonder. Even more, they demanded and also laid the foundations of a better and more just post-war society and were, albeit sometimes a little unwillingly, prepared to pay for it.

For many younger people the history of two struggles against the Germans is something that they believe ought to be forgotten. We are, after all, now members of the European Union, which has worked to create an ever-growing harmony with our neighbours, the like of which has not been seen since the times of Charlemagne. That we have been at peace with the rest of Europe for over fifty years is something to celebrate but modern Europe would never have been created without the blast of the two intensely destructive wars and the chaos which ensued after the last shot was fired. And what of the Sheffield area and the part played by its men and women of the steel industry during two world wars?

If ever a nation owed so much to a couple of generations, then this nation owes it to those of our parents and grandparents.

Bibliography

Barnett C., *The Audit of War* (London: Macmillan, 1986)

Barnett C., *The Lost Victory* (London: Pan, 1995)

Binfield C., *History of the City of Sheffield* (Sheffield: Sheffield Academic Press, 1993)

Calder A., *The People's War – Britain 1939–45* (London: Jonathan Cape, 1969)

Churchill W. S., *The World Crisis* (London: Thornton Butterworth, 1923)

Fairfax R., *The Blitz* (Brough: Agency Video, 1994)

Hardy C., *Sheffield at War* (Sheffield: Archive Publications, 1987)

Liddell-Hart B. H., *History of the First World War* (London: Cassel, 1970)

Phillips M. and Potter J., *Artist in Arms* (Durham: Pentland, 2001)

Stevenson J., *British Society 1914–1945* (London: Penguin, 1984)

Marwick A., *The Deluge* (London: Macmillan, 1965)

Scott P., *Vickers a History* (London: Weidenfeld & Nicolson, 1962)

Taylor A. J. P., *English History 1914–1945* (Oxford: OUP, 1965)

Walton M., *Sheffield, its Story and its Achievements* (Sheffield: Sheffield Telegraph & Star, 1948)

Notes

Chapter 1

1 Miscellaneous newspaper articles, Vol. 24, p. 118. Sheffield City Library.

2 A. D. Stacey, *A Historical Survey of the Manufacture of Naval Armour by Vickers, Sons and Co. and their Successors* (Sheffield: Unpublished, 1960) pp. 12–18.

Chapter 2

1 M. Phillips and J. Potter, *Artist in Arms* (Durham: The Pentland Press, 2001) p. 95.

2 Amongst that number were father and son, Emerson and Albert Dalton, the author's great-grandfather and grandfather who, like so many, carried on a tradition of whole families working for the same employer. The author's father would carry on this family tradition of working for Cammell's in a later conflict, albeit under its post-merger guise.

3 Miscellaneous newspaper articles, vol. 24, p. 113. Sheffield City Library.

Chapter 3

1 A. Marwick, *The Deluge* (London: Macmillan, 1965) p. 103.

2 J. Stevenson, *British Society 1914-1945* (London: Penguin, 1984) pp. 71–2.

3 *ibid.*

4 *ibid.*

5 W. S. Churchill, *The World Crisis* (London: Thornton Butterworth, 1923) p. 139.

6 *Artist in Arms* pp. 139–42.

7 P D Scott, Vickers – a History (London: Weidenfeld and Nicolson, 19620 p. 105.

8 *ibid* p. 105.

Chapter 4

1 These instructions ordered that two motor cyclists were to go to the following entrances to the City, previously protected by barriers at night and:

a) extinguish all lights in the vicinity

b) warn locals to remain under cover, extinguish lights, and keep doors closed and windows shrouded

c) watch all motor vehicles entering or leaving the City

d) investigate all cars using lights calculated to be serviceable by the enemy

Sheffield City's entrances were situated at:

Manchester Road at the junction with Rivelin New Road
Rivelin Valley Road near Walkley Bank Road
Far Lane, at the junction with Wadsley Lane
Middlewood Road at the junction with Leppings Lane
Wood Lane at the junction with Malin Bridge
Parkside Road at the junction with Penistone Road
Sheffield Lane Top
Shiregreen
Sheffield Road, Tinsley
Meadow Hall Road near Jenkin Road
Main Road at Handsworth Bridge
City Road at the junction with Standhouse Lane
Gleadless Road at Newfield Green
The junction of Derbyshire Lane and Cobnar Road
Chesterfield Road tram terminus
Abbeydale Road (South) at Beauchief
Ecclesall Road (South) at Bents Road
The junction of Ringinglow Road and Common Lane

Chapel Lane at Brookhouse Hill
The junction of Redmires Road and Crimicar Lane
The junction of Ben Lane and Dykes Lane
Moonshine Lane at Norwood Lane
The junction of Longley Lane and Carr Lane
Rivelin Valley Road at New Bridge
Loxley Road (just within the City boundary)
Cottage Lane, Ringinglow

2 H. Tatton, *Essays on Sheffield History and Places* (Sheffield: Unpublished, c.1920) Sheffield City Library.
3 *ibid.*

Chapter Seven
1 Left Wing Book Club, *The Strength of the Nations* (London: Gollancz, 1938) p. 68.
2 Clyde Alloy was the only company represented on the committee which was not based in the Sheffield area.
3 G. Tweedale, *Steel City* (Oxford: Clarendon Press, 1997) p. 303.
4 The author's father, who worked at English Steel Corporation during part of the war, spent a year or so before his call up into the RAF, firing machine-guns at test armour plates for the Spitfire.
5 Directors' Reports 1941, Sheffield City Library.
6 *British Society 1914–1945*, p. 448.

Chapter 8
1 E. N. Simmons and E. M. Sessions, *Jenkins of Rotherham* (York: Sessions, 1956) p. 64.

Chapter Nine
1 A. Calder, *The Peoples War – Britain 1939–45* (London: Jonathan Cape, 1969) p. 275.
2 C. Barnett, *The Audit of War* (London: Macmillan, 1984) p. 169.

Chapter Ten
1 R. Fairfax, *The Blitz* (Brough: Agency Video, 1994).

Chapter Eleven
1 A. Calder, *The People's War – Britain 1939–45* (London: Jonathan Cape, 1969) p. 275.
2 C. Barnett, *The Audit of War* (London: Macmillan, 1986) p. 169.